BEYOND WORDS

Nonverbal Communication in the Classroom

83959

JAMES J. THOMPSON
Department of Educational Media
College of Education, University of South Alabama

CITATION PRESS ~ NEW YORK ~ 1973

Library of Congress Catalog Card Number: 72–98009
Standard Book Number: 590-09560-8
Copyright © 1973 by James Thompson.
All rights reserved.
Published by Citation Press, Library and Trade
Division, Scholastic Magazines, Inc., Editorial
Office: 50 West 44th Street, New York, 10036.
Printed in the U.S.A.

BEYOND
WORDS

CONTENTS

WHY NONVERBAL COMMUNICATION?

Verbal communication is one of the most studied of human activities. At every level of schooling, from first grade through college, students are required to learn the structure of written and spoken language. Until they have mastered verbal language, students are not considered truly educated. Nonverbal communication, on the other hand, is one of the least studied of human activities. Nowhere at the present time is it considered important enough to be included in the basic curriculum of public schools. Yet when humans communicate, as much as eighty percent of the meaning of their messages is derived from nonverbal language. The implication is disturbing. As far as communication is concerned, human beings spend most of their time studying the wrong thing.

Human communication cannot be reduced to words alone. If it could, humans would have few communication problems. Telephone, radio, and television carry the human voice to the most remote corners of the earth; yet in this age of instant communication, incredible as it seems, the term "communications gap" has become commonplace. Why? Perhaps because human beings are basically nonverbal creatures who have merely learned to speak. They do not trust words. Traditional linguists have distorted beyond all possible reality the importance of verbal language in human interaction.

Conflict frequently arises when people believe that their verbalizations should be accepted at face value by other people. Of all the channels of communication available to humans, however, verbalization probably carries the least weight. Humans communicate with their entire bodies, and in situations of deep, personal meaning and importance, the body languages are more to be trusted than words. Words count for very little when they directly conflict with the silent languages of the body. Thus people may talk and talk, but until their nonverbal behavior agrees with their words, a credibility gap, not a communications gap, will exist.

Nonverbal messages are difficult to identify and analyze because they are frequently sent and received below the level of conscious awareness. Since these are the messages that govern most human interactions and their consequences, however, there is little choice in the matter. They must be studied, for here are the networks humans trust. Here is where the basic human dialogue occurs.

Since midcentury the serious study of nonverbal communication has attracted researchers from many different disciplines. Anthropologists, sociologists, psychologists, psychiatrists, and other students of human behavior have coined new words to describe the areas of human communication they are investigating. Clusters of embryonic sciences have grown up around their efforts. The extent and complexity of human communication is at last coming to light, and the implications for teachers are important enough to merit serious consideration.

The primary purpose of this book is to synthesize for the classroom teacher recent findings in human communication and, where applicable, to point out their significance for classroom teaching. Because of the newness of the data from these new fields of study, quite possibly many implications for teaching and learning have been overlooked. That really doesn't matter. In the long run, teachers will themselves determine what is of value to the successful practice of their profession. A mere beginning is intended here.

A secondary purpose is to encourage the teacher to become more than just a consumer of new information. To create new data is the ultimate contribution. The classroom is a living laboratory in human communication and behavior control. What better setting to study young people interacting with all the variables inherent in the social and educational processes? The artificiality of the laboratory and the difficulty in generalizing from rat and pigeon behavior to the human situation has reduced the importance of this type of research. In back of everyone's mind lurks the suspicion that the best planned research design that works well with monkeys could be turned upside down by intelligent human students who enjoy breaking the rules of the game. Human behavior is so unique that its exact analog in the animal realm simply does not exist.

A teacher should be a student of human communication, and the classroom is his laboratory. The field ahead is wide open, and opportunities to make a significant contribution to human knowledge are available. This book will provide a framework for organizing data and will offer some directions and guidelines to assist teachers in investigating human communication in the classroom.

PERSONAL
SPACE

Suppose you are seated at one end of a cafeteria table and another person seats himself at the far end. His message to you is clear: "Do not disturb me." If he had wanted to socialize, he would have sat closer to you. He has used space to send you a message. The manipulation of space to send messages from one person to another has been called *proxemics* by anthropologist Dr. Edward T. Hall, who founded the scientific study of space language.

Animals that live together, including humans, require space in which to move, eat, sleep, work, and socialize. Proxemics proposes to describe and investigate how they use space as a rudimentary language system to pass information back and forth. The classroom is a unique kind of space. It is a contrived human setting in which teacher and students are expected to live together for many hours each day and to learn certain competencies and acquire specific information.

But the human student is not a computer. Information cannot be programmed into him. The computer is a docile machine, but the student is a living, acting, resisting, wary human being. So the teacher's task is exceedingly difficult. Not only must he know exactly what to teach, he must also devise a methodology and create an environment conducive to learning. The latter tasks are most difficult to perform successfully, since they involve an operational knowledge of human behavior and its meaning in the classroom. It is to these aspects of teaching that proxemics may offer some new insights.

As work progresses in the study of space language, one recurring observation is evident. People use space as a buffer between themselves and other people and things in the environment. When individuals encounter someone or something pleasant, they reduce the space between themselves and the object. If the encountered person or thing is not pleasant, they increase the space. It is this addition and subtraction of space that gives observers cues and clues to making inferences about people's attitudes at any particular moment.

Naturally, some responses are more evident than others. When a teacher crosses a room to greet a student he likes, his reduction of space is easily seen. When he leans back in his chair at the approach of a student he does not like, however, the small increase in space may go unnoticed by casual observers. The students in both cases have probably noted the actions subconsciously and assigned meaning to his behavior. In time they will conclude that teacher does or does not like them. And no matter what the teacher says to the contrary, they will believe his behavior and not his words. Whenever there is a conflict between what is said and what is done, people believe behavior, not words. Nonverbal behavior, because it usually occurs subconsciously and is therefore not easily manipulated, is an authentic indicator of one's attitudes, values, and feelings.

Human beings belong to a class of animals that has been labeled "non-contact." Animals in this category usually maintain some space between themselves and other animals of the same species. Horses, dogs, and many other animals belong in this classification. Strictly speaking, the label "non-contact" is misleading because all animals permit body contact at certain times. But a non-contact animal's tolerance for skin contact is low compared with "contact" animals such as alligators and parakeets that tolerate continuous body contact with others of the same species.

Even within the same species, however, tolerance for contact may vary to some extent. For example, among human beings observation leads one to believe that children have a higher tolerance for body contact than adults and that females have a higher tolerance than males. Nevertheless, human beings shun continuous body contact and are most uncomfortable in situations where it is unavoidable. It can be said that every person maintains a small space barrier between himself and the world and only certain favored people are permitted to penetrate this barrier for short periods of time. But even they must eventually depart, leaving the individual encapsulated in his own, private space bubble.

From an early age humans learn the significance of space as a barrier between themselves and other people and events. Parents teach their children formally ("Don't stand so close when you talk, Johnny!"), and through imitation children teach themselves informally

("Mommy sets the plates *this far* apart.") many of the useful spatial concepts needed to understand and be understood by others. When children enter school, classmates and teachers continue this education, much of it taught and learned subconsciously, until finally they learn the important concepts of human spacing. From a social point of view, this kind of information may be among the most important learnings of children's lives. For example, if they do not learn arithmetic well, this deficiency becomes a relatively unimportant matter once children leave school. But if they do not learn how close to stand to people when conversing with them, this deficiency could affect the quality of their entire lives.

Why humans maintain this space barrier between themselves and others is a question that has not been answered to everyone's complete satisfaction. Part of the answer may lie in the human being's method of collecting information from the environment. Humans constantly probe the environment for useful information that is fed into their central and autonomic nervous systems through inputs that have not yet been fully identified. The five traditional sensory inputs (hearing, smelling, tasting, touching, and seeing) do not account for the reception of certain kinds of information that is routinely monitored by the brain, for example, bodily movement, posture, a sense of weight, hunger, nausea, and many other critical sensations. Obviously, there are more than five sensory inputs. Just how many, no one seems to know, but estimates run as high as fifty.

To monitor this welter of information efficiently may require a zone of neutral space around an individual. The human eye, for example, cannot focus correctly if objects are held too close. Perhaps humans maintain a space barrier as a sort of staging area where certain kinds of information are detected, sorted, and then transmitted to the brain for analysis. Prolonged body contact may overload some inputs, deprive others, and distort information flowing into others. Humans need diverse kinds of information. When it is not forthcoming, they grow uncomfortable and confused. Experimental subjects held in total isolation in a completely unchanging environment soon began to hallucinate and lose contact with reality.

The important point for the teacher to consider is that human space barriers should not be violated indiscriminately. Crowded rooms, halls, tables, and benches where students are forced to rub against each other continuously must surely inhibit learning. There is too much body heat, too much noise, too many odors, too much to see and to touch. To expect students to concentrate in the midst of this sensory bombardment may be impossible.

Crowding, jostling, and lack of elbow room induce stress and anxiety. In other animals crowding leads to hostility, and hostility leads to aggression, which in turn leads to killing. Killing, of course, provides more space for the survivors. While evidence certainly cannot be generalized indiscriminately from lower animals to humans, neither can it be dismissed out of hand. Many classrooms may be stress-inducing because students are not provided with adequate space in which to gather the information they need to perform comfortably.

While most crowded civilized humans have not yet resorted to killing each other, they have developed a kind of ritualistic "killing" that is just as effective. They withdraw into their own cocoons and ignore everyone else around them. Each person becomes completely indifferent to the "non-persons" pressing in on him. Consider the hordes of unhappy people riding crowded subways and buses in large cities during rush hours. Jammed together, eyes cast down or in their newspapers, unsmiling, unfeeling, they endure in silence the total violation of their personal space until they reach their destinations. Only indifference to others makes this terrible crush of bodies endurable.

Unfortunately, such indifference sometimes leads to tragic outcomes. People have been robbed, beaten, and murdered while others looked on indifferently. In crowded cities what happens to a "non-person" is a matter of little concern. A "non-person" has no feelings, no identity; he cannot suffer. Therefore, it is considered all right to look away and not become involved.

The code of a crowded city dweller is simple: (*1*) look down and you will not see, (*2*) in a crowd, become an inconspicuous pressure and refrain from making human noises and movement, (*3*) do not become involved. The innocent out-of-towner who does not know this code and who persists in behaving like a human being while riding a crowded subway is an embarrassment to everyone around him.

What is more alarming, children apparently are learning the same behavior. A recent study presented evidence that as children grow older, they show less concern for other children in distress. Younger children from kindergarten to second grade expressed a willingness to go to the assistance of other children who called for help, but this helping behavior disappeared in the upper grades. How much of this indifference is due to crowded conditions in cities, schools, and homes is, of course, an unanswerable question at present. Yet it is a question that should concern teachers deeply.

The territorial behavior of humans is a neglected area of study. In fact, more is known about the territoriality of birds. How does a student stake out his ground? How does he defend it? What are its dimensions? What does he do if his territory is invaded by other students or a threatening teacher? How much privacy does a student need and how does this need change with age and maturity? Even rats must have some privacy. Yet in the public schools the amount of privacy students are permitted ranges from none to very little. How does a student manipulate the space around him to send a teacher messages? What do these messages mean?

By increasing and reducing space people provide important clues to understanding how they feel about other people and events in their immediate environment. The television salesman who holds his sponsor's product at arm's length is probably saying nonverbally that he doesn't think much of it. The three-year-old who clutches her doll tightly to her bosom is saying that it is one of the most precious things she owns. The student who won't approach a teacher is saying that he doesn't like the teacher or is afraid of him. The school principal who sits at the back of the auditorium during a class play is saying that he is not particularly interested in the play. All are using space to send messages.

Because space seems empty and neutral, it is often difficult to comprehend its real dynamics. Space is for acting in, for running in, for living in, for fighting in, for working in. A few great architects such as Frank Lloyd Wright have understood this. Wright said, "Form follows function." Unfortunately, the traditional architects who usually design homes and schools seldom follow Wright's dictum. When they circumscribe space with wood, stone, and plastics, the esthetics of *seeing* frequently takes precedence over function. They design beautiful looking homes that inhibit living and functional looking schools that inhibit learning. People do more than *look* at space—they *behave* in it. The quality and quantity of space shape their behavior. Cried Hamlet, "O God, I could be bounded in a nutshell and count myself king of infinite space, were it not that I have bad dreams." Many "bad dreams" are frequently a direct result of the "nutshells" in which people are confined by architects.

Consciously and subconsciously, a person is aware of everything that happens in his microspace, everything, that is, that he is equipped to sense. Have you ever worked at your desk, engrossed in grading an assignment, when you heard a student walking toward you? Perhaps you kept on working. Then, marvelously, at precisely the right instant, not a fraction of a moment too soon or too late, you looked up. While you worked, a primitive computer deep inside you monitored the student's approach. At exactly the right instant, it triggered you to action. So wondrously precise are these ancient computers, clocks, and compasses of animals that they regulate vital biological functions of humans, summon the salmon upstream to spawn, and send the giant sea turtle a thousand miles to a lonely beach at precisely the right time. Where they are located and how they work is one of the most baffling mysteries confronting the life scientists.

What goes on in a person's microspace determines

much of what he is and what he will become. So important are these close-in events that if a human is deprived of certain vital information during the first few years of life, he will undoubtedly suffer deficiencies and handicaps from which he will find it most difficult to recover, if indeed he can recover at all. For example, in medieval times court jesters were in great demand. Some parents imprisoned their children in odd-shaped cages causing their small bodies to grow in grotesque and deformed ways. The children were then sold as jesters.

The manufactured jesters of medieval times were no more grotesque in body than some of today's children who are deformed in mind and spirit by the cages of their early biospace. A child cannot grow up in the dirt and din of an urban ghetto or in the suffocating poverty of a migrant workers' camp without being bent and twisted into a social jester. Dr. René Dubos, noted American bacteriologist and health authority, claims that man is the product of his biospace. It is time to study this space, to learn how humans use it, how they collect information from it, how they change it, and how it changes them.

Intimate Space

The space closest to a person is his intimate space. Among mature adults in American culture body contact and extremely close body positions signify intimacy. The intimate zone extends outward from a person in all directions to approximately eighteen inches. Intimate space is reserved for loved ones, for occasional contacts with family members, and perhaps for a few close friends. Friends and family, however, must not remain there too long, especially if there is body contact.

At eighteen inches, the physical presence of another person is overwhelming. Three dimensional vision is lost. Faces are blurred and distorted and appear monstrously large. The breath is easily detected—warm, moist, and laden with information about the other person. So breath-conscious are Americans that even intimate friends hesitate to get within breath range of each other. If circumstances necessitate whispering, they judiciously turn their heads or shield their mouths with their hands. Not lightly in our culture does one breathe on one's friends.

Body heat is another source of information when someone enters a person's intimate space. Ordinarily the sensing of another's body heat is objectionable. Just what this thermal information is all about and why it is so objectionable are questions without satisfactory answer at present. Yet people do not object to and frequently seek a specific individual's body heat at certain times. What kind of information do they receive, and what do they do with it?

Needless to say, intimate spacing seldom occurs voluntarily in public. When elderly adults sometimes speak of the "shameless" behavior of teenagers in public places, usually they mean that these young people accept and invite intrusion into each other's intimate space. A similar objection is sometimes raised by wives at cocktail parties. A wife may instantly dislike another woman. On closer analysis, the other woman may have invaded or may simply hover on the fringes of her husband's intimate space. In American culture intimate space is reserved for intimate business. To disregard this rule is to invite social criticism.

This fact, perhaps ironically, tells something about not being "loved." A child who is not loved may seldom or never be held close by another person. He does not receive certain kinds of information that most humans seek from and give to other special humans. An unloved child has never been permitted to get close enough to breathe on someone or to feel another's breath. He has never felt another's body heat or another's heart beating against his own. He has never looked into another's face so closely that it has melted away in a blur. There is an entire class of information that has been denied him. Therefore, he is less human, less social. There may be certain times in his life when he will make mistakes and certain tasks he cannot perform well simply because he has never been "loved."

Teachers who invade students' intimate space at will are intruders. They are not welcome. Furthermore, the message that the student receives from this intrusion is insidious. It says, "You are not a person; you are a non-person. Therefore, you are not entitled to intimate space. As your teacher I may enter and depart at leisure. You have no feelings in this matter because non-persons do not have feelings."

It makes little difference to students how often or how fervently the teacher verbally acknowledges them as unique individuals. Students know better because whether he realizes it or not, the teacher's behavior has eloquently communicated his real feelings. Intrusion into one's intimate space is such an unsettling and disturbing experience that police interrogators sometimes use this technique to break down a suspect's composure. It is equally disturbing to students.

If a teacher is ever in doubt about how students feel about his proximity to them, he may look for certain signs. Among the first signals of unwelcome intrusion are rocking, leg swinging, or tapping. This is a student's way of saying, "You are too close and I am uncomfortable." If the teacher continues to ignore these signals, students may close their eyes and withdraw their chins chestward. This is the final desperate plea. The message is, "You do not exist. Can't you see I have obliterated you? Now go away."

Just as a teacher expects students to respect his intimate zone, he must respect the intimate space of his students. Regardless of age, each student is entitled to control the space immediately surrounding his body. The perceptive teacher will spare students the anxiety of willful intrusions.

Individual Space

An individual's personal zone extends from eighteen inches outward to approximately four feet or arm's length in all directions. This is the distance reserved for good friends and for discussing personal business. At this distance friends tell each other their troubles.

Three-dimensional vision is restored. Body heat cannot usually be detected, and, of course, a person is out of breath range. This is a comfortable distance to discuss a student's personal problems. Some students may prefer to remain on the outward boundary of the personal zone. If a teacher attempts to move closer, they may move back and reestablish the boundary line. A teacher can take his cues from the student. He will permit a teacher to move closer as he learns to trust and like him. If a teacher forces his way in prematurely, the student will become ill at ease.

For teachers of interracial and intercultural classes, the problem of spacing is especially perplexing. Personal spacing is to a great extent culture-based. Some cultures, for example Latin American, permit a much closer spacing than do North American or European. A teacher of students of Latin American origin may find himself backing away to reestablish his own personal boundaries. These students may appear aggressive; the teacher may feel that they are crowding him. He may find also that they modulate their voices differently. They speak louder. And they like to maintain direct eye contact, something that Europeans and North Americans seldom do. The natural reaction is to move back, especially if the teacher is a woman dealing with a class of high school juniors or seniors.

But of course the teacher must not move back. Part of the business of teaching—and of international diplomacy, too—is to learn about and be able to operate within another person's cultural frames of reference. An American teacher must be culturally versatile, even though he has received little or no training in this important aspect of teaching. There is no "proper" distance to stand and no "proper" way to modulate the voice outside of specific cultural contexts. What a teacher thinks is "proper" is merely customary. That is the way he was taught. People from other cultures were taught differently, and they believe their way is "proper."

Black students, Mexican students, Puerto Rican students, Indian students, Eskimo students, even Irish, Italian, and Jewish students will handle spacing the way their parents taught them. Given enough time they may learn the "American" way. But they must have an opportunity to learn, and above all, they must see a social or economic advantage to learning. Some may refuse to learn new ways; cultural preferences must be expected and respected.

Perhaps it would be helpful to point out to the female teacher that she can expect her male students to handle space somewhat differently than female students. Boys generally wish the teacher to stay well outside of their intimate and personal space. Perhaps this is due in part to their conditioned suspicion of all schools and teachers. Approximately eighty-five percent of all elementary school teachers are women, and men hold a bare majority in high schools. To many boys, schools are worlds of women, and they find it increasingly difficult to get a fair deal. Studies have shown that boys who score high on masculinity tests receive the lowest grades. There are some authorities who maintain that American schools are determined to feminize boys by rewarding feminine behavior and punishing masculine behavior. Be that as it may, it is a fact that seventy percent of all student suicides are boys; three out of four mental breakdowns among students are boys; and three out of four of teachers' problem cases are boys. Perceptive teachers may wish to take a second look at the plight of young men in our schools.

The culturally versatile teacher should be able to operate with small cultural, racial, and sex differences. Some of them may confuse, annoy, and confound him until he learns more about them. But the good teacher, like the good physician, must be able to rise above his own discomfort and hold the welfare of his clients before all else.

Arm's length is also a good husband–wife distance for discussing the utility bill that wasn't paid or for deciding which child must give up his room to grandma when she arrives next week. When one person enters another's personal zone, he expects him to say something personal. Unless a teacher has private business to transact with a student, he should remain outside of the student's personal space.

Social Space

Beyond the personal zone another kind of distance, called social space, has been identified. As the name implies, this is the area reserved for casual friends and acquaintances, for co-workers, and for general socializing. It extends from four feet outward to about twelve feet. Since this distance is unusually large (on a microspace scale), it has been subdivided into close social space (four to seven feet) and far social space (seven to twelve feet). Naturally, these boundaries are flexible to some degree, although the overall dimensions are fairly stable.

In its close phase, social distance encompasses impersonal activities. This is the distance teachers usually maintain from each other at faculty meetings, and the distance parents usually keep when they visit a teacher in the classroom. If a teacher asks the principal of the school a personal question at this distance, he would probably move to personal distance before answering. Students expect the same courtesy from their teacher. Discussion of personal affairs such as grades, conduct, dress, or activities should be carried on with individual students from personal distance, even though it is often more convenient for the teacher to do so from social distance.

In its far phase, social distance requires certain kinds

of adjustments so that two people may communicate with each other. For example, each must watch the other's face. Without raising the voice level, it is difficult for a person to be heard at ten or twelve feet. Therefore, the listener resorts to visual cues. He watches the eyes and lips, combining visual with auditory information to receive a complete message. To carry on a conversation at social distance therefore requires eye contact.

It is possible at this distance to continue work in the presence of another person. An office secretary, for example, may continue to work as long as the boss does not approach within seven feet or less. If he moves into the close phase of her social distance, however, she will probably look up to see what he wants. Teachers frequently encroach upon the close social or even the personal distance of students and expect students to continue work. Teachers may even forbid students to look up or otherwise take notice of their presence. They are asking the impossible, of course. When an authority figure such as a teacher invades a student's social or personal space, the student cannot ignore him. The teacher may bully a student into keeping his eyes on his work, but rest assured his attention will be on the teacher until he retreats to at least seven feet.

Since these areas of personal and social space are all around the student, approaching him from the rear merely compounds the problem. He cannot see the teacher, so every sensory input will be turned on full to determine where he is and what he is up to. Based on animal studies, there is evidence that subordinates "freeze" at the close approach of a dominant. Teachers may witness a similar phenomenon in their classrooms.

As the teacher approaches a student, his presence is so overwhelming that literally, the student "freezes." Until the teacher moves away or his attention is diverted elsewhere, the student is practically helpless. In graduate schools, candidates for advanced degrees are sometimes closely flanked by faculty members during their oral examinations. This seating arrangement is almost certain to guarantee a poor performance by the candidate.

Teachers who have developed the exasperating habit (to students) of walking around the room while students are taking an exam, merely distract students and make their task more difficult. A teacher may best help his students during this stressful period by sitting unobtrusively at his desk and minding his own business.

The far phase of social distance is an ideal distance for family room socializing. Husband, wife and children may engage or disengage from each other at will. At this distance teachers may work at their own particular tasks —grading papers, for example—without interfering with each other and yet be able to drop in and out of on-going conversations whenever they wish.

Public Space

The outermost zone of an individual's microspace is called public space. It extends from twelve feet outward to approximately twenty-five feet at its close phase, and from twenty-five feet outward as far as the individual can perceive at its far phase. At the close phase of public distance, the structure of speech usually changes. It becomes more formal. A person lectures more than talks, and his tone of voice and gestures support his formal posture.

Many university professors—and some high school teachers—manage to maintain this distance between themselves and their students. Consequently, their classes are generally formal, and some students may feel that the teacher is cold and distant. This impression may be false, but if a teacher insists on making public utterances from a distance of fifteen or twenty feet, it is difficult for students to perceive otherwise.

The far phase of public space is for strangers, those countless people who move into and out of one's life daily. In ways known and unknown they affect the quality of a person's life and his relationships with people closer to him. A teacher who does not mingle, literally, with his students will remain a stranger to them. As a stranger his influence is limited. But as a friend, who knows where a teacher's influence could end? And the key to it all is to move a little closer to students in space as well as in spirit.

Critical Space

There is another kind of space to consider. Thus far the microspace of an individual has been described in terms of his interpersonal relations. Now space will be redefined according to a new set of criteria.

If family, friends, and strangers were the only people who entered a person's microspace, life would indeed be more pleasant. Unfortunately this is not the case. Occasionally one has to deal with threatening intruders. These are not merely people whom one dislikes. They actually pose a threat to one's person or who are perceived as posing a threat. When an intruder enters that area surrounding a person called the critical space, the tendency is to attack the intruder in self-defense.

The size of an animal's critical space is proportional to the size of the animal. The critical space of a mouse is much smaller than the critical space of a dog. The animal is located at the center of its critical space, which according to some authorities extends 360° all around, and according to others, is more elliptical than round. The latter group points out, for example, that a person can tolerate the closeness of strangers at his sides more than at his front or rear. Work with various animals of many sizes, including captive animals in zoos and circuses, confirms the idea that any animal tends to fight if his critical space is invaded by threatening intruders.

The critical space of a mature adult human is approximately three feet. In other words, the human stands at the center of an imaginary ellipse or circle whose radius is three feet. Any human or animal who enters this circle with the intent of doing physical harm, or who is capable of doing harm, will face immediate, defensive action. There is some additional evidence that the critical space of violent people is not only elliptical but extends a greater distance to the rear. If further evidence verifies this observation, clinicians may be able to identify and perhaps work with violence-prone people at an early age.

The identification and description of critical spacing may shed some new light on the violent behavior of some students. If a student perceives a teacher as an enemy, someone who is capable of doing him grave, physical harm, then he may not tolerate the intrusion of the teacher into his critical space without taking violent countermeasures. Humans are extremely complex organisms, and undoubtedly the interplay of many variables makes their behavior at any given instant not entirely predictable. Nevertheless, it is safe to predict that it is risky for a teacher to threaten violence, and even riskier to attempt to carry out the threat. The number of teachers being struck by students is growing. How much of this is actually triggered by threatening teachers who press students is not known. The problem is even more acute when students and teachers of different races and cultures must spend hours, days, and months together in the same room. Not enough is known about human spacing, and territoriality and their racial and cultural variants at present to prescribe specific courses of action for the teacher. Based on what is known, however, common sense provides one good rule of thumb: do not invade the critical space of students intending to do physical harm. If you do, you must expect the student, regardless of age, to strike back.

Flight Space

Big or small, docile or ferocious, most animals would rather run than fight. But running takes time and space. Generally speaking, the bigger the animal, the more time and space it needs. An elephant must keep enough distance between itself and dangerous intruders to overcome initial shock and inertia and provide a reasonable margin of safety. Therefore, the flight space of an elephant is great.

Flight space is that area beyond the critical space of an animal where the animal will flee at the approach of a threatening intruder. Of course, if the intruder continues to pursue and manages to close the distance between itself and its quarry, as soon as its critical zone is penetrated, the pursued animal will probably turn and attack the pursuer. Given sufficient time and space, however, most animals will flee at the approach of a threatening stranger.

Some students flee at the approach of a threatening teacher. This is a normal and instinctive reaction and should be expected. If a teacher believes a student should stand his ground while he is approached in a threatening manner, the teacher may be asking the impossible. Furthermore, to demand that a student voluntarily approach a teacher for the purpose of receiving physical punishment is unreasonable. Many students comply with such demands, however, and one may wonder what effects these unnatural behaviors have on their total personalities. Even a dog will not consistently approach its master for a beating.

Corporal punishment, a rather fancy name for inflicting physical violence on students, is gradually disappearing from the American school system. Perhaps educators are becoming more civilized, or perhaps students are simply growing bigger and stronger. At any rate, it never was much of a deterrent for some students, as many teachers know. To punish physically is an animal-like behavior. The teacher who employs it invites an animal-like response. Humans are not so long out of the water and down from the trees that they have forgotten to meet force with counter force.

Social Isolation

If crowding triggers hostility and aggression, isolation breeds anxiety and neurosis. Just as animals cannot be herded together into crowded enclosures without adverse reaction, neither can they be kept so far apart that they lose complete contact with other members of the same species. In their natural state, animals need to see, smell, touch, and hear other familiar animals, or they will grow nervous and irritable.

To say that man is a social animal is less than helpful until some of the important characteristics of human socialization are defined and described. Wolves are social, and so are lambs, birds, and many insects. If the important modes and mechanisms of socializing can be isolated and identified, however, then scientists may better understand why animals that live cooperatively, including human beings, behave as they do. Any in-depth study of the socialization process inevitably focuses on communication.

Students of communication, as they probe deeper into the inner workings of all goal-oriented organizations of animals, people, ideas, and even machinery, are beginning to comprehend the importance of communication in the maintaining and survival of those organizations. Without a continuous flow of relevant information, logical things tend to break down. Unless a television set receives the signals trapped by the antenna, the set will not function. Without a continuous flow of information between a teacher and his students, the class, as a purposeful organization, will begin to degenerate. Communication keeps the bits and pieces of an organization in touch with each other so that they work harmoniously to perform a common task.

Communication is the biochemistry of the social sciences. It is the fundamental base of conditions and propositions upon which the socialization process with all its myriad variations is built. Without communication, cooperative living would not be possible, and without cooperative living, societies, groups, and institutions would cease to exist. Social isolation deprives the individual or the group of information necessary for maintaining positive goal behavior.

Applying these concepts to the school situation, it is easy to see that no classroom can be truly "self-contained," an island by itself, and long remain a meaningful entity within the larger school system. A teacher cannot socially isolate his classroom from the rest of the school or bring the world into his classroom; these are myths. A classroom is simply an enclosure of limited dimensions bounded by walls, ceiling, and floor. It supports a limited number of activities and a limited range of behaviors. Instead of trying to bring the world into a tiny classroom, it would perhaps be more useful to seek ways in which to help the class break into the world. Teachers should make extensive use of libraries, learning centers, resource centers, social rooms, and other communal facilities. They should permit their students to come and go as much as possible and encourage them to seek questions and answers beyond the contrived environment of one small room. The universe, after all, is infinite. These teachers may not be popular with the sort of school administrator who feels secure only when the sixth-grade class is in the sixth-grade room. But their students will appreciate them.

Perhaps, too, we should look at the social isolation of many neighborhood schools. Walls, chain link fences, and red tape cut them off from the events and people they were built to serve. When the morning bell rings, students are not permitted into the neighborhood nor are the neighbors allowed to enter the schools. When vandals come, students cheer, and neighbors look the other way because the schools belong to neither. Per-

haps it is time to give the schools back to the neighborhoods, to involve the neighbors in the life of the school
and the school in the lives of the neighbors. This is
easier said than done, however, because it will involve
curricular, instructional, and architectural changes that
traditional education did not foresee.

The study of personal space, its extent and variety,
has opened up a brand new area of research. What has
been discovered so far is probably a mere speck in a
universe of phenomena waiting to be discovered.

FOR FURTHER READING

Esser, Aristide H. *Behavior and Environment: The Use of
  Space by Animals and Men.* New York: Plenum
  Press, 1971.

Fast, Julius. *Body Language.* New York: Evans, 1970.

Hall, Edward T. *The Hidden Dimension.* New York: Doubleday, 1966.

————. *The Silent Language.* New York: Premier Books,
  1959.

Sexton, Patricia. "How the American Boy is Feminized."
  Psychology Today, vol. 3, no. 8, Jan. 1970, pp. 23–9.

Somner, Robert. *Personal Space.* Englewood Cliffs, N.J.:
  Prentice-Hall, 1969.

Thompson, James J. "Instructional Communication." *Nonverbal Communication.* New York: Van Nostrand
  Reinhold, 1969, chapter 11.

"Would Your Child Respond to an S.O.S. Signal?" *ERIC/
  ECE Newsletter,* vol. 4, no. 5, July 1970.

WORK
SPACE

The microspace of an individual includes the space in which he works. Naturally, working space and personal space at times become so intermingled that they cannot be separated. The area immediately surrounding a student's desk, for example, is both his work space and his personal space. In his work space, however, a student is expected to perform special tasks that may require certain tools and spatial configurations. A student carries his personal space with him, but his work space usually remains static.

Ordinarily designing working and living space is a highly specialized task. Consider for a moment the job of a curator of a large zoo. Through a stroke of good fortune he has the opportunity of acquiring a pair of rare and exotic animals. Now he must prepare a place for them in his zoo. What will he do? First, he will probably get in touch with experts who have studied the life style of this particular species. Based on their recommendations, he will construct a habitat in which the animals will best thrive. Temperature, topography, privacy, light, diet—all these factors will be carefully considered. When all preparations are completed, he will install his animals. Is he finished? Indeed not. He will observe the animals carefully for many months, perhaps years, to determine that conditions are, in fact, favorable for their health, safety, and general well-being.

It is a fact that some animals in zoos receive more considerate and intelligent attention than students in some schools. Construction of the student's work habitat is frequently planned by persons who have little knowledge of human learning or of the kinds of spatial configurations and furnishings that will support and facilitate learning.

Because humans are highly adaptive organisms, in the past men assumed that it was less expensive to force other men to adapt to work environments rather than adapt the environments to human capacities and potentials. In the short run, it was less expensive. Mass production is an excellent example of this concept. The human worker becomes an adjunct to, a part of, the machine. He is paced by a conveyor belt, and he may work no faster or better than the weakest link in the work chain. There is little room in this sort of operation for insight or ideation, the kind of work humans seem to do best. The worker is an automaton; his human characteristics are seldom used on the job. Henry Ford once said that the ideal factory worker would be a trained ape.

True, mass-produced goods are inexpensive. In the long run, however, mass production from the human point of view may be an expensive failure. Human workers find little challenge on the job. They reserve their best efforts for off-the-job activities. Absenteeism, shoddy workmanship, and the spiraling demands of organized labor are the human worker's way of saying that as a human being he is not being used well. Consequently he demands and obtains more money. The more people learn of human behavior, however, the more they are beginning to understand that money alone cannot compensate a worker for the loss of his humanity. The only intelligent answer is to change the work environment so that it challenges and supports human potentials.

Similarly, in the short run it may be less expensive to construct schools from model sets of blueprints, to purchase stock furniture from the lowest bidder, and to assign students to specific desks in specific rooms at specific times to perform specific tasks. This is mass education, but in the long run it, too, may be an expensive failure. The signs are everywhere evident in students' frustration and boredom, in the failure to educate significant numbers of students, in the drop-out rate, and in the clamor for accountability by parents, governments, and students themselves.

But if educators are to change what they have, to what should they change? Given the constraints of the real world—the thousands of existing schools, the limited amount of money available for education, the kinds and numbers of teachers presently on the job, and the meager extent of knowledge in the behavioral sciences —what would be a reasonable response to the problems of creating a more enlightened work environment for students? Part of the answer may be learned from the curator of the zoo. The school environment must be adapted to the learning and living styles of human students.

The field of study grappling with man's relationships to his work environment is called, in the United States, *human factors engineering*. In some European countries it is known as *ergonomics*. Human factors came into prominence in scientists' attempts to design an environment in which astronauts could function effectively and efficiently on their journeys into space. Human factors engineering strives to capitalize on unique human capacities, yet provide for human weaknesses and inconsistencies. Manned space ships, for example, enable men to function as critical, curious, and intelligent participants during most of the flight. But at certain times, such as moon descent or earth reentry when enormous quantities of data must be acted upon in split seconds with little margin for error, computers take over. It is an ideal arrangement. Men are free to wonder and worry, to speculate about the unknown, and to act upon unforeseen problems arising in real time. This is what men do best. Machines handle routine decisions based on known data. That is what machines do best. The entire environment is engineered in such a way that the kind of work space available, and the amount, are consistent with human factors and the job to be done.

Now the teacher may wonder, "What does this have to do with me? I'm not training astronauts. I'm trying to teach biology to ninth-graders." True, but human factors engineering has nothing to do with space technology, *per se*. It is merely a way of adapting a work environment to human beings, wherever it occurs. Manned space flights simply provide spectacular evidence that the technique pays off in terms of successful task completion.

Ordinarily the builders of schools do not approach the work environment of students in this way. Chances are, the school and classroom in which a teacher works were planned by architects and school administrators who gave little thought to the quirks and aberrations of human student behavior or to the real demands of learning itself. With the exception of highly specialized work areas such as science laboratories and band rooms, school architects assume that the same kind of space will serve everyone. Whether he teaches history, literature, or social studies, a teacher is assigned to a rectangular enclosure with a certain number of chairs and given a desk for himself. He and his students must adapt to this environment. Other than the size of the chairs, there is little difference between a first-grade classroom and a university classroom. In terms of the kinds of students to be accommodated and the nature of their tasks, is this not a strange situation?

Where is there evidence that most subjects are best taught to most students in essentially the same way? That students learn best when seated at desks? That a rectangular classroom is the best spatial configuration for group learning? That uniform blocks of time serve each subject equally well? That doors and windows are in the best possible places? That the color on the walls, the tiles on the floor, the shape of the desks, or the height of the ceiling have no direct bearing on what and how students perform? These and countless other unfounded assumptions were made by the planners of most schools and classrooms. That teachers and students have functioned under these conditions merely points up their extraordinary adaptability. That these conditions frequently do affect the teacher's work and his students' progress is beyond reasonable doubt.

Although schools have been in operation for a long time, educators are newcomers to a human factors approach to school construction. This means that billions of dollars have already been invested in existing facilities that cannot be wiped out and built anew. Most classrooms are rectangular. Most students sit at desks. Most school principals assign a certain number of students to each room under the supervision of one teacher. To ignore these existing constraints would be unrealistic. Therefore there seems to be two avenues of action open to educators:

1. Determine as precisely as possible the effects of existing work environments on student performance.
2. Based on this information, change what can be changed to improve the situation, and in the future apply what has been learned when new facilities are in the planning stage.

The basic reason for schools is students. Educators need to study them so that they may build schools around students, and so the students, in turn, may perform to the best of their abilities. The remainder of this chapter will be concerned with some effects of existing classroom conditions on the behavior of students. Information in this area is relatively scarce and frequently disjointed, but it is all we have. We need more and better information.

Student Seating Patterns

Most teachers have their own notion of what constitutes

the ideal seating arrangements of students. Some teachers assign seats. Other teachers permit students to make the decision, and still others have not given much thought to the matter, one way or the other.

If a teacher assigns seats, even though this arrangement may facilitate classroom management, he is cutting himself off from a valuable source of data. When students are given the choice of selecting their own seats, they will not usually select randomly. Selection may be conscious, or more often subconscious, but it is a rational decision based on information about himself, the teacher, the course, and how the student happens to feel about school at a particular moment.

Many teachers have undoubtedly noticed that the same students consistently seat themselves toward the front, middle, or rear of their classrooms. Other students may prefer the walls or corners. All of them, by their seating patterns, may provide teachers with valuable information about themselves.

Dr. Robert Sommer, Professor of Psychology at the University of California at Davis, has conducted numerous studies on the effects of classroom settings upon attitudes and behavior of students. He has gathered evidence that in the typical straight-row arrangement of most classrooms, students in the front row participate more in on-going activities than students in any other row. A teacher may safely assume, then, that any student who seats himself in the front row wants to become involved. There is some speculation that increased eye contact with the teacher may account in part for this active participation, and undoubtedly eye contact is a contributing factor. For example, a student who usually sits toward the rear may enter late and take the nearest available seat in the front row. Suddenly, for the first time all year, the teacher is amazed to find him contributing to a discussion. Direct eye contact with the teacher may be the source of his motivation.

These cases, however, are the exception. More often, front row students tend to sit there regularly. They are the live wires, and if a teacher is not careful, he may find himself playing to them and neglecting the rest of the class.

Contrary to what one might expect, the second-best participating row is not the second row, but the students along the side walls. Isn't that strange? As yet, no one claims to know why, but there it is. Perhaps these are students who are quite capable but who need the security of a wall at one side before they are willing to risk themselves. Current studies show that with the exception of the front row, students along the side walls participate more than any other group of students in the room. Notice, also, that students along the walls have the second-best eye contact positions in the room.

Back row students probably wish to maintain substantial distance between the teacher and themselves. As noted in the previous chapter, people tend to increase the space between themselves and unpleasant people and events in their immediate environment. The teacher may expect these students to participate little, but he might wonder why they do not. After all, they are also part of the class.

In the center segment of the room participation tends to be greater and, with the exception of the wall row, drops off significantly on either side. Again, why students seat themselves in the center is an intriguing riddle at the moment. There are no hard and fast "rules" and "laws" of seating, however. Studies merely show tendencies. A teacher's own experience may not support the current data. If not, here is an opportunity to begin collecting new data.

If nothing else, these studies point up the need for spatial freedom in the classroom. There will be times when students want to participate and other times when they will not. They will be more comfortable and more productive if they have the freedom to move forward when they feel interested and retreat when they feel insecure and out of sorts. Limited as a teacher is to his own classroom, he should encourage his students to use all of the space available to them in the most productive way. He should permit students to move about with freedom, and once they have decided on a particular location for the time being, their choice ought to be respected.

Some teachers, sensing that there is something inhibiting about a front desk position and static rows of chairs, attempt to get more class participation by "opening up" the seating pattern. They arrange students' desks in horseshoe or open square configurations. Based on limited evidence, there is a tendency in these kinds of arrangements to get more participation but from fewer students. So if wider participation is the goal, straight-row seating seems to be the best arrangement.

In a small seminar-type class, a teacher can expect the most active participation from the students directly in front of him. He will probably notice that participation drops off noticeably on either side. Another point of frequent concern to the teacher of a small class is whether to use tables or regular desk chairs. If the goal is active, widespread participation, he will probably get better results with tables. Students seated at tables talk more than students seated in desk chairs. Of course, quantity by no mean implies quality!

When teaching a small class or group, there is a temptation on the part of the teacher to seat himself as close as possible to the group. Students frequently are uncomfortable and intimidated by teachers who make these overt, friendly gestures. Personal space is a precious commodity. Animals will fight for it, and people resent intrusions into it except by invitation. Teachers sometimes get the notion that to influence their students, to be most persuasive, they must close in on them. But the evidence points the other way. A teacher will be more persuasive at a distance of fourteen or fifteen feet, and least persuasive at two or three feet. If he happens to be that lucky teacher in a hundred who naturally attracts students, they will invite him closer. Ordinarily, however, a teacher must be exceedingly careful not to crowd his students regardless of how well intentioned he is.

In small group work, most students usually prefer to leave vacant the chairs on either side of a teacher. There is good reason for this. Students will be more open to his persuasion and leadership and will feel less inhibited in responding to him. If he insists that students occupy these seats, or if he seats himself in a group when adjacent chairs are occupied, the students seated on either side of him will probably remain silent throughout the entire session. As has already been noted the near presence of dominant authority figures may cause subordinates to "freeze."

Studies of student seating patterns are relatively new. Most of the information that will be of most use has yet to be discovered. The trick is, of course, to ask the right research questions. Dr. Robert Sommer reports an interesting example. A study of four thousand classrooms revealed that half the children with chronic infections were found in the left rear quadrant of the room; that is, the quadrant usually closest to the windows. If the researcher had not asked the right question, this useful information would have eluded him. And by the way, assuming that this observation is true, why not take advantage of it?

Why not reserve the left rear quarter of the room for those students who wish to be temporarily uninvolved? Adults know that one does not have to be violently ill to wish to be left alone. There will be class periods when, for one reason or another, a student may not wish to become involved. But in school, where can he go? If he cuts class, he is penalized. Since this student probably will not do much work anyway, why not permit him to retire to the rear, without penalty, with the understanding that the teacher will respect his temporary disengagement and will not disturb him? Teachers may expect some abuse of the privilege, but the general results might prove beneficial.

Students seem to have reasons for sitting where they do. Do not expect them to verbalize these reasons. Most of the time they will not consciously be aware of them. When a teacher chooses a tie or jacket of a particular color in the morning, could he verbalize his reasons? Yet he, too, probably has some subconscious rationale. It is best to assume that student behavior is logical. As an interested researcher, a teacher should seek the logic.

Privacy

Privacy is one of the most precious privileges of an open society. Privacy is so important to North Americans that invasion of another's privacy leaves one open to legal action. People fence their houses, drape their windows, and lock their doors. Even within the same family, the right to individual privacy is taken for granted. Most parents would not think of bursting into their teenagers' bedrooms without first knocking. A wide open society can be tolerated only as long as there is a place where, screened from other's eyes and ears, a person may relax and be alone.

Taking into account the highly personal nature of learning, isn't it amazing how little privacy is afforded students? From the moment he enters school in the morning, the student becomes public property. There is not a single place where he may retire from public view, not even for a few minutes. There are the rest rooms, of course, and many students take advantage of them for a few stolen moments of relaxation. But even in the rest rooms, there is no guarantee that his privacy will be respected.

If educators think of student privacy at all, they usually think of it in negative terms. They are accountable for the student; therefore they must know where he is at all times. Schooling is also a socializing process. A student must learn to get along with and relate to others. What better way to insure that this will take place than to keep him in constant contact with others? After all, these are public schools, not private. Privacy in the public schools is an alien notion. But is it?

Psychiatric workers once held similar views about social therapy. In treating severe cases of social withdrawal, they reasoned that contact with others ought to draw out withdrawn patients. But a surprising thing happened. As the number of beds in a ward increased, patients became less social. Eventually each patient withdrew to his own bed and chair, and social intercourse was cut off completely. Patients who were most social, who spoke with the staff, and took the most interest in social contacts were found in private and semiprivate rooms.

Certainly psychiatric data must be shifted with care from the hospital to the classroom, yet the concept is so fundamental, so basic, and so completely ignored in schools that one is entitled to wonder and worry. In American culture only animals and infants—and students in public schools—are permitted no privacy.

Younger students frequently and ingeniously devise their own privacy. It is not uncommon to find third- or fourth-graders studying under tables and desks or behind doors. Apparently they are permitted more spatial freedom than their high school counterparts, who are generally restricted to their own chairs. Try to make sense out of that! Complete withdrawal is sometimes the only recourse open to a student surrounded by classmates and teacher, constantly watched and frequently harassed by authority figures. Many students turn to fantasy and become psychological drop-outs.

In a society that values privacy so highly, it is difficult to justify to students their lack of private space. A perceptive student has already noticed the relationship between space and status. More and better private space goes to those people with the highest status. This observation is reinforced constantly on television, in the movies, even in the very school in which the student works. The school principal has his own private office, probably larger than that of the assistant principal. The superintendent undoubtedly has the largest and most elaborately furnished office of anyone in the school system. The more important a person is, the more and better private space he commands. A student is given no private space. Where does that leave him?

It is time for educators to abandon their plans for super auditoriums, super lunch rooms and super social rooms and begin to think of student privacy. Today's student is a different breed of human being from his parents. His world is up-tight, crowded, noisy, violent— an orgy of stimulation. Yet educators keep offering more stimulation instead of the peace and quiet he craves. Colleges continue to spend small fortunes building and furnishing elaborate dormitory lounges instead of making bedrooms, where students spend most of their time, more comfortable. Even in their rooms, few students study at the desks provided. Most students are more comfortable on the floor, in bed, or in lounge chairs. Further, studies show no difference in learning regardless of how students study. Why then do building planners continue to supply desks? Why do they continue to build larger lounges? Obviously in some cases they have lost touch with today's realities. They are attempting to foist on students a world that no longer exists, if indeed it ever did exist.

But how can teachers manage to provide privacy in crowded classrooms? Privacy is not a matter of square footage but of screening. The most crowded-looking slum sometimes affords more privacy for people than many new apartment complexes. Boston's West End, for example, was considered a slum and was consequently razed to make way for new apartment buildings. Lives were disrupted, people were moved, and many were made homeless and unhappy. Too late, housing authorities discovered that the West End was not a slum—it was just slummy-looking. Working class people had added on all sorts of home-made barriers and screens to give themselves some privacy. Actually, most of the people there treasured their neighborhood because they were close to friends, relatives, and work. It had taken years to create the sort of screening that housing authorities called a "slum."

Simple barriers—carrels, bookcases, shelves, and portable panels—if placed with care, will break up open spaces in the classroom. Freedom to move about, to seek corners, or just to turn one's back will afford some relief. But the teacher's attitude will be of most help. Privacy is as much an attitude as it is a spatial arrangement. The perceptive teacher who is willing to concede to a student the right to disengage and retire without penalty to a seat of his choosing has already made the most important commitment—the human one.

Students may now be living in the twilight of the big classroom and the garrulous teacher. More and more, educators are accepting the view that learning is a highly personal business that must be carried on in a highly personal setting. Technology offers some relief in this respect, but until the profession is able to educate teachers who can bend technology to their purpose, there will probably be only limited success. Nor are the learning factories of the performance contractors the answer to private and personal learning. Information technology may expedite the process of information gain, but the information gained has little utility outside the human dimension, which gives it meaning and purpose. Humans learn not because information exists, but because they see human meaning and purpose in what they learn. Man is not yet a cyborg, and he should not be educated as though he were one.

Work Groups

With the possible exception of the fine arts, human work is frequently a group undertaking. In the United States people seem to be particularly attached to the "team effort." The size of the team or group is usually determined by the kind of work to be done. Not much attention is paid to the social aspects of work groups except as they affect production. A number of people are assembled, assigned subtasks, and a finished product is expected to emerge. Not infrequently, however, industrial management has had to face up to the notion of work as a social enterprise. In the 1950s workers went on strike in some of Great Britain's newly automated factories, not for money but for more time to socialize. Automation had increased the distance between work stations and made it difficult for workers to exchange social pleasantries. They struck for better social working conditions.

In the "natural" state, however, people tend to resist grouping. That is, if the way people group themselves of their own volition is to be accepted as a criterion, groups in the real world are hardly groups at all. Studies indicate that people usually congregate in two's. Groups of three people are sometimes encountered, but groups of more than three are rare. A teacher may verify these results for himself. The next time he visits a large shopping center, airport terminal, or other place where people congregate, he may note the number of people in each group he encounters. Even when a large group gathers to see a person off at an airport terminal, for example, the group usually splinters into smaller groups of two's and three's. The implication for the teacher is quite serious. His usual idea of a "small" work group of students may be a large and unnatural social group.

Everything considered, teachers should reexamine their grouping practices. Unless there are important reasons for doing otherwise, perhaps "natural" groups of two or three students ought to be the rule. Since larger groups run counter to what people ordinarily do, would it not be safe to assume that larger groups impose a strain on social relationships, which in turn may affect the group's efficiency? The kind of group opinion and "togetherness" sought by many teachers simply does not exist. People are individuals and will resist all efforts to lump them into groups where they lose most of their individual identity. True concensus is an occasional phenomenon. Even if each student does not or cannot speak for himself, he will certainly think for himself.

The typical classroom was never intended to accommodate many small groups of two or three students. It will take a great deal of ingenuity on the part of a teacher and his students to rearrange classroom space for small group activity. Yet the results in terms of active and meaningful participation could well be worth the effort. It is well to remember, however, that the social isolation of small groups is not desirable either. For example, scattered groups of two in a large auditorium are liable to feel cut off and out of contact with each other.

Such groups will gradually move closer together. As a room becomes larger, people tend to come together. The answer is screening. If somehow a teacher can manage to screen one group from another and provide minimum sensory barriers, density becomes less important.

When grouping students for classroom work, some teachers believe in manipulating group membership for the best possible mix of interest, aptitudes, socioeconomic background, or race. The limited evidence available, however, does not support an underlying assumption that proximity will breed familiarity and friendships. In new neighborhoods, where few people know each other, proximity does tend to increase the likelihood of friendships at the outset. Next door neighbors usually become friends. But the friendships may not last. As the neighborhood matures, people tend to seek out other socially compatible people, even though they may live blocks apart. The same phenomenon may occur in the classroom. In spite of a teacher's efforts and good intentions, he may find his students grouping themselves according to ability, race, or interests. In genuine social situations his interference probably would not be appreciated. But when it comes time for work, there are considerations that ought to take precedence over friendships.

The Coleman Report (see bibliography at end of chapter), for example, offers some firm guidelines for the deliberate mixing of black and white students in the typical racially integrated school. According to this evidence, the achievement of black students is highest when the proportion of blacks to whites is forty percent or less. If a teacher attempts to maintain this ratio when grouping students for work, he may meet with resistance. Understandably, students do not wish to be separated from their friends and supporters. But in this case, group manipulation may be justified. Gains in achievement, however, must be weighed against the kind and amount of social trauma they induce. Not enough is known about the effects of stress, anxiety, and social disruption on human behavior at present to prescribe hard and fast rules. Teachers should proceed with caution.

In the final analysis, one resource directly related to student achievement is the quality of one's classmates. New buildings, better equipment, or flexible schedules cannot compensate for the lack of contact with other students of broad and varied backgrounds. This is the most formidable argument for total integration in schools and has been so used by the courts. Contrived mixing seems to be an efficient way at present of helping underprivileged students overcome deficiencies of substandard schooling. Not surprisingly, then, lower-class black children learn more if they attend a middle-class, mainly white school than if they attend a lower-class, mainly white school. The social problems inherent in this kind of predetermined mixing, however, often seem to defy solution. Nevertheless, there is a real danger of becoming a severely polarized society unless a reasonable amount of social trauma is endured to achieve long range balance and equity in public education.

Teachers need to take a second look at small group work in their classes. Groups are probably not small enough in some instances and not mixed enough in others. Hanging over any efforts they might make, however, is the emotional, imponderable social variable. It is a wise teacher indeed who knows when to allow his grouping practices to run with the social grain and when to run against it.

While grouping to achieve racial balance is a problem of grave concern to many teachers, other teachers are equally concerned about maintaining balance between the sexes in their student work groups. Most teachers' practices in this area have been largely intuitive. Not much in the way of practical information has been available.

Dr. Jonathan L. Freedman of Columbia University has completed a study that may have some practical implications for teachers. He recorded the behavior of groups of men, women, and mixed-sex groups under conditions of crowding. He reported that groups of men responded negatively to crowding. They became suspicious, combative, and highly territory conscious. Women, on the other hand, responded more positively. They tended to become more friendly and intimate. Of particular interest to teachers, however, was his discovery that under the same crowded conditions, all the effects of density, both good and bad, disappeared in mixed sex groups. He concluded that, contrary to what has been noted in the previous chapter, not all crowding is necessarily bad. It depends on who is crowding whom.

The Work Setting

Work usually takes place in a special setting designed to facilitate the task. The golf pro performs outdoors. The medical intern may work in the emergency room of a large hospital within easy reach of people, equipment, and facilities he needs to support his practice. Students work in schools. In each case the work setting creates expectations about how people are to behave in that particular setting. The intern is supposed to act calmly and efficiently, going about his work in a swift, methodical fashion. The golf pro is expected to behave like a gentleman sportsman. He may dress casually but always neatly. He is not supposed to throw his clubs, shout at spectators, or heckle his opponents.

People entering work settings are also supposed to behave according to a set of expectations. When a person enters a church, he is expected to behave reverently. When he enters a bank, he is expected to speak quietly and respectfully in the presence of money. In each case, the physical setting is itself a key to eliciting certain kinds of behavior. Thus the environment creates sets of expectations with which most people comply.

As work environments, schools, too, create expectations, although frequently teachers are hard pressed to define them or defend them. A case in point is the trend to eliminate windows in schools. Windowless schools are more efficient in terms of heating, upkeep, and reducing outside noise. On the other hand, windows provide human beings with a greater variety of optical stimuli. There is some evidence that humans are most comfortable when they have freedom for occasional idle scanning of a visual field broader than the narrow confines of a work setting. Therefore windowless schools will create certain kinds of expectations, and schools with windows will create others. Exactly what kinds of expectations are elicited in either case has not yet been fully identified. Obviously, however, the decision to eliminate windows ought not to be based solely on administrative or architectural factors, since it changes the environment drastically, which in turn will affect student expectations and performance.

Even the very tables and chairs in a classroom affect

student behavior. A table is shared space. Each student at the table mentally "stakes off" a part of the table as his own. Here he deposits his belongings. Each occupant is expected to confine his clutter to his own immediate area. Pushing out beyond his own space into another's, without permission, will usually cause a student's neighbor to feel uncomfortable and imposed upon. The offending overflow will probably be pushed right back, perhaps subconsciously, by the neighbor.

Further, the shape of a table may either facilitate or impede the process of mentally sectioning the table. A round table, for example, is difficult to divide into equal spaces. Consequently people with a strong sense of territoriality may feel frustrated when working at round tables. Young children are in this category. Work tables for the primary grades, whether in classrooms, libraries, or lunch rooms, should be square or rectangular. Old folks, too, have a low tolerance for territorial ambiguity. They feel most comfortable at square or rectangular tables where "their" space has a higher degree of permanency.

Round tables are sometimes popular because they eliminate the responsibility of designating who should sit at the head of the table. At least King Arthur must have thought so. This is a consideration not passed over lightly. The head position seems to carry with it a certain intrinsic propriety. In simulated jury selection studies, a striking trend was noted to elect as foreman the persons who sat at either of the head positions.

The implications here should not be lost on teachers who wish to improve the image and credibility of certain students. If head positions possess this built-in image booster, certainly some experimentation might be interesting. Generally, people from higher socioeconomic classes tend to seat themselves at the head positions. Usually they talk more than others at the table, and other occupants believe that head people make the most significant contribution to the work. Here is an excellent opportunity for the curious teacher to determine just how far he can push the intrinsic propriety notion of head positions before the concept begins to break down. Perhaps he could assign head positions to students who might benefit from an opportunity to have leadership thrust upon them.

The family dining room seems not to be immune to the "pecking order" inherent in rectangular-shaped tables. If dad sits at the head of the table unchallenged, there is little doubt about his leadership role. If mom has claimed the bottom position, however, she may be in competition with dad for leadership. If dad and mom sit cater-cornered, the chances are good that both are secure in their marriage roles.

If children are permitted to select their own positions at work tables, they may provide a teacher with useful information about themselves. As a rule, children who are cooperating with each other tend to sit side by side. This is a favorite position of children, especially girls. Unlike adults, young children will not usually prefer to sit opposite each other, although as they grow older, the tendency to do so increases.

It is not unusual to find pairs of children who insist on competing. These young competitors will usually be found at the corners of rectangular tables. If a teacher assigns separate tasks to two children, or if each child wishes to work without interference from the other, they will probably sit cater-cornered.

Leadership is a significant variable when attempting to analyze the task behavior of students working at tables. In general, when a strong leader exerts his influence, participants speak to their partners in adjacent seats. If a strong leader does not emerge, people will usually direct their comments to those sitting opposite. Thus a moment's study of conversational patterns could provide a teacher with information about leadership or the lack of it, in many table groups.

In summary, the work behavior of people can be analyzed if researchers discover why people behave as they do. This is difficult because human behavior to an outside observer sometimes appears to be illogical. Human beings will rearrange furniture, tools, techniques, and some of the most efficient procedures according to sets of human whims and values that seem to defy all known logic. People will resist attempts to force them into rigorous patterns of behavior and thwart efforts to impose upon them a system of logic that is incompatible with their own.

In public assemblies the last rows of an auditorium usually fill up first, to the chagrin of the speaker. In restaurants and cafeterias single diners refuse to sit together but will occupy entire individual tables. In parks, two people will thoughtlessly close off a large bench to others by seating themselves at both ends. In doctors' and dentists' waiting rooms some patients will stand rather than occupy the middle seat of a three position couch. In church, worshippers frequently attempt to close off entire pews by seating themselves at end positions. In short, people defy architects and designers by outwitting or outwaiting them, by passive resistance and active defiance, through cunning, by accident, and through sheer determination. People will come in the "out" door, walk up the "down" stairs, drive the wrong way on one-way streets, and dial wrong telephone numbers. A man-proof environment, one that does not severely penalize people for these uniquely human idiosyncracies, is the only possible response to the frequently unpredictable behavior of human beings.

Throughout the range of human behavior there seems to be a persistent drive to stake out territory. From the youngest to the oldest, people are more comfortable when they have defined the limits of "their" space and where their territorial rights are respected. This trait is not limited to humans, of course, but is evident throughout the entire animal kingdom. Birds mark the limits of their territory through song. Bears claw the bark from tree trunks. Wolves urinate on the ground to mark their territory. In his excellent book, *"The Territorial Imperative,"* Robert Ardrey has explored this concept in depth.

Even when humans must absent themselves from their territory, they may leave behind markers that other humans respect. The fence around a person's house is obvious. When he goes off on vacation, not only do his neighbors honor his boundaries, but they will see to it that others do not trespass. Have you ever held a seat for a stranger who just happened to sit beside you in a theater? So strong is the sense of territoriality that seats may be held for hours. In airports, libraries, and bus depots a magazine or book will usually reserve one's seat. And a sweater, jacket, or other personal item may hold the seat for days.

Regarding schools as work environments, the time is approaching when the word "school" may have little meaning in the usual generic sense. Facilities will be built around the process of schooling and will probably take many forms from store-front private enterprises and home study courses to large government supported institutes. All will have one element in common: the environment, including work space, will be built around the enterprise they are meant to support and the students they are meant to serve.

The design of teaching and learning facilities will no longer be left to the whim and caprice of architects and administrators or the well-intentioned but sometimes self-defeating policies of school boards. The productivity of students, their peace of mind, and the growing body of information now at hand will all dictate that instructional facilities be built around the behavior of students and the kinds of work they are expected to perform.

New ideas about the role of the school in the life of the community and the role of students within the school are ready to be entertained. The social isolation of schools and the wisdom of high chain link fences to keep the neighbors out and the children in are being questioned. Educators are beginning to wonder what would happen if they moved the work environment of students closer to the work environment of adults—if they moved schools into industrial buildings, downtown office spaces, and suburban apartment complexes. What effects would such joint occupancy have on the lives of students and adult workers?

Even the landscaping of schools must serve a functional purpose. Every tree and bush should be planted to give shade, to provide privacy, and to reduce noise levels. But functionality need not preclude beauty. The successful reduction of high noise levels through intelligent landscaping is an excellent case in point. Many urban and suburban schools are plagued with excessive noise, usually from nearby road traffic. Today people are extremely conscious of noise as a form of environmental pollution. In the vicinity of schools, noise is intolerable. Noise, however, is more than a nuisance—it is a menace. Excessive noise may bring on heart attacks, may affect the mental and physical stability of unborn infants, and is rapidly reducing the hearing acuity of many young people.

Careful planting of trees may not only provide a beautiful view, but may also reduce drastically the noise of commercial traffic. If trees are planted close together, seventy-five feet of planted ground between the school and the highway will reduce noise by about sixty-five percent. And if seventy-five feet of ground is not available, even a few trees will help.

Noise illustrates the precarious balance of things in the working environment. The complete absence of noise may also adversely affect human efficiency. Some new office buildings have been so acoustically sealed that the ensuing deadly silence disturbed office workers and interfered with their concentration. When "white noise"—an electronically created sound resembling the roar of a distant waterfall—was transmitted through the air conditioning system, efficiency levels returned to normal.

Within new schools there will be a distinct trend toward more variety in work space for students. In the early sixties, infinite flexibility seemed to be the goal. In the seventies, however, extreme flexibility is viewed as neither practical nor desirable. The inefficiency and impermanence of folding partitions, sliding doors, and disappearing walls have cancelled out much of their utility. Instead, a greater variety of permanent working space seems to be a better answer. Some structural flexibility is still desirable, of course. But if the demands and outcomes of student tasks are carefully analyzed, and if the concept of personal, individual learning is taken seriously, smaller and more intimate permanent spaces may better meet student needs.

The seventies will undoubtedly witness a healthy trend toward participatory planning by architects, administrators, teachers, and students. Architects are themselves pushing this innovative approach. They have begun to accept the cold fact that a school building may be an artistic creation, but it is also a structure to facilitate work, just like a bank or a hospital. To ignore the idiosyncracies of the users—the students and teachers—may in many instances be a fatal omission. A school is not a piece of sculpture nor a series of ordered boxes. It is human work environment.

In new schools, "open" teaching will be commonplace. There will be freedom to move and time to think for students and teachers both. There will be social rooms, private cubicles, small conference rooms, laboratories for experimentation in the sciences, including the social sciences, a variety of learning stations, and a variety of teaching modes. A school will be a busy place, and traffic will be heavy all day long. Hopefully, teachers and administrators for these new schools are somewhere being trained.

FOR FURTHER READING

Alland, Alexander. *The Human Imperative.* New York: Columbia University, 1972.

Ardrey, Richard. *The Territorial Imperative.* New York: Atheneum, 1966.

Coleman, James S. "The Children Have Outgrown the Schools." *Psychology Today*, vol. 5, no. 9, Feb. 1972, pp. 72–5.

Freedman, Jonathan L. "The Crowd: Maybe Not So Madding After All." *Psychology Today*, vol. 5, no. 4, Sept. 1971, pp. 58–61.

Mangin, William. "Squatter Settlements." *Scientific American*, vol. 217, no. 4, Oct. 1967, pp. 21–9.

Meister, David. *Human Factors*. New York: Wiley-Interscience, 1971.

Propst, Robert. *High School: The Process and the Place*. New York: Educational Facilities Laboratories, 1972.

Racial Isolation in Public Schools: A Report of the U.S. Commission on Civil Rights (The Coleman Report). Washington, D.C.: Government Printing Office, vols. 1 and 2, 1967.

Rosenfeld, Albert. *The Second Genesis*. Englewood Cliffs, N.J.: Prentice-Hall, 1969.

Sommer, Robert. *Personal Space*. Englewood Cliffs, N.J.: Prentice-Hall, 1969.

Thompson, James, and Akin, Linda. "Individual Study Spaces for Young Children." *Audiovisual Instruction*, vol. 14, no. 7, Sept. 1969, pp. 38–40.

Winkel, Gary H. "The Nervous Affair between Behavior Scientists and Designers." *Scientific American*, vol. 3, no. 10, March 1970, pp. 31–5.

COLOR
IN THE CLASSROOM

Henry Ford offered his customers any color automobile they wanted—as long as it was black. But that was a long, long time ago, as color merchandising goes. Today a major automobile manufacturer may offer 650 standard color combinations or any kind of color customizing a customer is willing to pay for. Color sells cars—and houses, dresses, cereals, boats, lamps, luggage, and vacations. This is a world of color, a world of impact reds and psychedelic pinks, icy blues and seductive lavenders. Color is confusing.

Schools are educating what is perhaps America's first truly color-liberated generation. Today's students grew up with Peter Max posters, color television, rock rhythms, and flashing lights. They may be the first nonverbal generation, too. Their vocabulary frequently seems not to keep pace with their feelings. When words fail them, students turn to movement, dress, music—and color.

Any study of man's microspace would be incomplete,

even invalid, without considering the color dimension. Color gives things form, and people react to color as much as to form or function. When a detergent manufacturer sprinkled red granules throughout his white soap powder, housewives complained that the detergent was too rough on their hands. He changed the color to yellow, and women said it was easier on the hands, but clothes were not as clean. Then he changed to blue, and the ladies said it was just right. Nothing had changed but the color of the granules!

If the traditional school administrator thought of color at all, it was in terms of maximum paint for minimum money. Schools cloaked themselves in washed-out institutional green. This monotonous color was a maintenance man's delight. One or two cans of touch-up served the entire school. Paint could be shuttled back and forth between schools with little danger of mismatching. This no-nonsense approach to school interior decoration undoubtedly saved taxpayers thousands of dollars. That it may have alienated thousands of students was not even considered.

School people, of course, tended to rationalize the subduing effects of their color scheme on students. The whole idea was to surround students with bland walls and stern furniture, to remind them of the task at hand, and above all, to avoid the appearance of anything in the architecture, color scheme, or furnishings that might even suggest the frivolous. Schools, like hospitals, prisons, and orphanages, were serious institutions intent upon serious business. They were places where the young served time until the state legally set them free.

Since they were seldom consulted, students tolerated what adults gave them. They learned to live in these drab buildings, to have some fun in spite of the dreary interiors, and, surprisingly, most learned what adults expected them to learn. Even when the paint was allowed to flake and mildew, even when their classrooms were denied the annual coating of institutional green, students learned. The shabbiness of the environment was seen only by the primitive eye of the subconscious, a minor irritant, but one that eroded students' confidence, pride, pleasure, and ability. A vital, interlocking piece of the environment had been allowed to deteriorate, and the results spread beyond immediate view.

Even the paint on the walls of classrooms may influence what and how students learn. Studies show that in some instances just repainting a classroom in traditional green may produce a measurable gain in class achievement. Paint in pleasant shades of warm and cool colors may produce an even greater gain.

The causal link between colors in the environment and specific kinds of behaviors has yet to be established to everyone's satisfaction. However, the case for planned color schemes for schools is pedagogically sound considering what is known about the effects of color on human behavior.

Color by chance, whim, misguided esthetics, or economy fails to take advantage of information already available. For example, some years ago it was fashionable to replace old fashioned gray slate blackboards with green chalkboards. Green chalkboards were supposed to be "easier on the eyes" and easier to read. The facts show otherwise. There is no substantive evidence that green boards are "easier on the eyes." Indeed, there is evidence that under normal classroom lighting conditions, green boards are more difficult to read because of the reduced contrast between the white chalk and the green board. They are just as difficult as slate boards to keep clean, and they have the added disadvantage of restricting color combinations and choices in the classroom. Obviously, some school administrators made decisions based on misinformation or no information at all. They instituted a major color change in the classroom environment without considering the implications of the change.

People today are color conscious, and their homes, schools, churches, and other public buildings reflect their new concern. In many instances, school administrators are calling in color consultants to help them plan functional decorations for schools. Of course, there are still schools where the principal's wife is the only authority consulted, but hopefully these are few.

Color is a language understood by the subconscious. How conscious behavior is shaped by this subconscious acquisition of information is not known completely. Enough is known, however, to warn administrators and architects to use color intelligently when it is a dominant part of the environment of any task-oriented group. A typical illustration may help underscore this point.

An eastern college recruited a large group of students from slum areas. They were given their own dormitory, and the college administration and faculty expected them to move in and begin to participate in the life of the college. This did not happen. The reaction of the students was largely negative. Frustrated and bewildered, the administration tried many new accommodations and arrangements without success. The behavior and attitudes of their new students were beyond the administration's understanding. As a last resort and after all other efforts had failed, the college called in a color consultant.

In outward appearance, the dormitory looked like a fort. To middle-class Americans used to living in stereotyped houses, the fort-like appearance of the dormitory would have been a welcome and exciting change. After all, how often does one get the opportunity of living in a fort? To the new students, however, most of whom had never seen a picture of a fort, the building looked like—and became—a prison.

The interior walls of the building were gray-blue, unpainted cinder block. From the college's point of view, the walls were certainly different. The texture of the block was architecturally interesting and provided an excellent and tasteful background for interior furnishings. Stairwells were unfinished concrete with the board marks left on the surface, giving an interesting, textural touch. Although this may have been new and seemed tasteful to the administration, the students had seen it all before in the damp basements of the tenements they had left.

The furniture was simple with clean lines. Tables and chairs were modern, slender, unpretentious, and easily moved about for cleaning. Unfortunately, most of the students were completely unfamiliar with this style of furniture. They had neither seen nor used anything like it before. Since they had no frame of reference to make judgments, they were dissatisfied and uncomfortable in their rooms. The crowning feature of the interior was red carpeting on the floor, which merely accentuated all the disturbing features of the building.

The consultant recommended more massive tables

and chairs upholstered in warm colors and patterns. Immediately the interior took on a more solid, stable, and comfortable look. He recommended colored draperies for the windows, which offset the drab, cinder block of the walls and lightened the whole room. Next he recommended that the red carpet be replaced with a more suitable one. With a few deft touches, the consultant had gone right to the heart of the problem and proposed solutions that worked.

At stake was the comfort and peace of mind of students threatened by environmental details that school administrators frequently consider hardly worth their time and attention. Yet until these human problems are resolved, academic problems and programs are hardly worth students' time and attention. One cannot expect a drowning man to consider seriously the nature of the universe, but set him on dry land and make him reasonably at ease, and he might become interested in other things beyond himself.

Vision and Color

What is really known about color? The study of color as a science began with Newton. Suppose by some miracle teachers were given the opportunity to attend a lecture by Sir Isaac Newton. Newton, a giant among giants, had one of the most fertile minds this species has produced, yet, to their amazement, teachers would discover that this great man frequently lectured to an almost empty room. Newton's students apparently had no way of knowing that their teacher was a genius. They cut his classes. This bit of information may provide some small comfort for unsung, harassed teachers everywhere.

In his laboratory in the year 1666, the twenty-three-year old Cambridge instructor allowed a beam of sunlight to pass through a prism. The prism spread the beam apart, and on the opposite wall appeared a rainbow-hued oval. He had demonstrated one of the most elementary, yet one of the most profound discoveries in all science.

In just a few seconds Newton invalidated theories of another revered man of science, Leonardo da Vinci. Da Vinci and others had thought that the color of an object was in the object. That is, the red of an apple was actually in the skin of the apple. The apple *was* red. Newton demonstrated that the molecular structure of the apple skin allowed all the various waves of light to penetrate the skin, except the particular wave length associated with red. This wave was reflected back, rejected, by the apple skin. The wave length entered the eye of a human observer to become red.

Color is not in an object, nor is it in the waves of light; rather it is in the eye and brain of the beholder. Yellow objects merely reflect the particular wave length associated with yellow and absorb all others. Therefore one sees yellow. Objects appear black when they absorb all the wave lengths, and white when they reflect all wave lengths. If one person says that a hat is blue and another argues that it is green, they are both right and both wrong. They are both wrong because the hat has no color at all; both are right because each brain is interpreting exactly what it sees through its eyes, and no two pair of eyes see exactly alike. If a person sees green, then green it is. Color is a sensation within the brain. It does not exist apart from a color-sensitive observer.

Just how humans see color is still very much of a mystery. There are a few respectable theories, each differing in some important ways from the others, but none of them explains to everyone's satisfaction the phenomenon of color vision. A layman is frequently disappointed when his eyes are easily fooled by optical illusions. But to the scientist working in color and vision, the miracle is that eyes manage to see anything at all, so complex and little understood is the process of seeing. Yet so sensitive is the human eye that it can detect a lighted candle fourteen miles away and see details on a landscape flooded by eight thousand foot candles of sunlight!

Evidence is mounting, by the way, that visual illusions are not caused by limitations of the eye or brain. Indeed, the opposite may be closer to the truth. These organs are so refined that they report all the possibilities based on available information. The eye alone has no way of ascertaining the weight, warmth, softness, or hardness of visual images. Thus in searching for or attempting to establish the reality of objects, frequently a number of different hypotheses are presented to the brain for consideration. Visual perception is essentially the selection of the most appropriate stored hypothesis based on current sensory data. Sometimes the hypothesis does not conform to reality, and the eyes are fooled.

For example, if the vanes of a windmill are viewed obliquely or directly from the side, they may seem to reverse direction spontaneously and frequently. Such perceptions are not caused by distortions of the retinal image. They are the alternative interpretations of the human brain, which is trying to "make up its mind" but cannot because incoming sensory data are ambiguous. So if anything, visual illusions merely point up the splendid precision and sensitivity of the human nervous system.

Color Preferences

Centuries before Newton, far back into antiquity, people used and responded to color. They adorned themselves, their dwellings, and their artifacts with paints and dyes supplied by nature. Some of these dyes, for example purple, were expensive to manufacture and were unavailable to common people. Purple garments became a sign of wealth and nobility and are so associated to this day. Because raw materials for making paints and dyes are found throughout the habitable earth, color is a universal phenomenon peculiar to all people regardless of race or color. Since the same dyestuffs were generally available to all, it is not surprising that certain colors kept recurring wherever humans settled regardless of the state of advancement of a particular people.

Red is one of these colors. It is a universal favorite, just as popular in America as in Africa and equally loved by the Sioux of the Dakotas and the Zulus of Natal. Today if you see a red sportscar, it could belong to a Chinese physicist, a Black dentist, or a Panamanian diplomat. If the human race has one common social denominator, it must be the love of color. Color cuts across race, age, sex, and culture and even bends back upon time.

Throughout the ages the function of color has been to adorn and to appeal to the emotions. Occasionally color served as identification—to identify one army from another, one house from another, or one's tools from another's. But in general, color was associated with human emotional states. Mondays were blue, lovers were blue or sometimes green with envy, cowards were yellow, sometimes people saw red, but much of the time they felt in the pink. Today color has the same emotional appeal, but a new dimension has been added. Color is being employed systematically to evoke or suppress human feelings and responses, and there are numerous associations, private and public, that are seeking ways to exploit human color sensitivity toward various ends. The age of behavior control through color is already upon us.

Housing developments use color extensively to create feelings of spaciousness and difference when, in fact, little spaciousness and few differences exist. It is common knowledge that urban and suburban space is dwindling. As space is used up, the cost of land rises necessitating smaller houses and less buffer space between neighbors. Even in areas of high density developers are able, through careful color planning, to make each house just a little different from its neighbors. By using just two roof colors, four siding colors, and eight trim colors, no two houses in a typical development of 144 look exactly alike.

Interior space is also at a premium. Every square foot must be utilized. No longer can special purpose rooms be unused for long periods. All are drawn into the living scheme of the house. The white kitchen of yesterday, off limits to everyone except the cook, is gone. Decorative colors on walls, appliances, and floors have opened the kitchen to family traffic. Today's kitchen is colorful, cool, and inviting.

Even bathrooms with their colorful fixtures have undergone profound decorative changes. Telephones matching the color scheme of a room are quite popular, in spite of their added cost. Apparently people are willing to pay the price for color. Sales on new color appliances have never been higher.

Within this context, then, color planning for schools is essential. The constancy of color in a student's daily life and his physical and psychological reactions to color make it imperative that teachers make color work for students rather than against them. Color is an essential part of the facilitating environment.

If a person with normal vision were shown a chart of color gradations he would be able to distinguish about 128 different hues. The human eye can make these fine distinctions, however, only when it is able to compare. In daily living it is most unlikely that one would encounter more than a fraction of this number.

Historically the most universally appealing colors are red, yellow, green, and blue. These colors and combinations of them are found on Egyptian artifacts, the banners of ancient Rome, the garments of medieval European nobility, in the paintings of colonial artists, and in today's supermarkets and department stores. Red, yellow, green, and blue are found somewhere in the living style of every known major culture and in every cultural past. The world's peoples may differ in size, race, politics, language, religion, diet, standard of living, and a hundred other factors, but there are four tough threads that have bound humans together and have withstood the passage of time and ideologies. They are just as strong today as they were five thousand years ago—color them red, yellow, green, and blue.

Color preferences change with age and maturity. Most

authorities seem to agree that there is a positive shift in preference from warm to cool colors as a child grows older. This shift takes place from age three to about age fifteen. Before the age of three, color preferences have not been firmly established, although there is evidence that during the first year color saturation and brilliance determine preference.

Kindergarten children will enter school with a built-in preference for red, yellow, or blue. Orange, a combination of red and yellow, is also a favorite color. These are the colors of childhood, warm, vibrant, and exciting. If children were permitted to decorate their rooms or buy their own clothes, these are the colors they would most likely choose. The perceptive teacher will subordinate his own color preferences to those of his young students. He will permit them to decorate in the colors that support and encourage the activities of childhood. Even a teacher's school wardrobe should be chosen with care to appeal to young children. Sometimes a teacher may find himself wearing to class styles and colors of clothing he would never wear off the job. This is the sort of useful dedication that gets results, however, in terms of rapport with children. Bulletin boards, posters, displays, and illustrations for young children should be decorated in the colors that appeal to them. Until a teacher manages to get students' attention, he cannot expect to accomplish much, and red, yellow, and blue are the colors that attract young children and with which they feel most comfortable.

Teachers of high school juniors and seniors may expect to see yellow begin to disappear from students' color preferences. It will probably be replaced by green. Green is a mature adult color and should be firmly entrenched in a student's color repertoire by the time he reaches college. In decorating the school environment of older students, their color preferences should be given priority over other considerations, including misguided esthetics.

Seasonal and special holiday colors will take precedence over usual preferences. At Christmas, green will be as popular in the kindergarten classroom as anywhere else. When planning the color schemes of classrooms, other important factors must also be considered, such as lighting, temperature, size of room, and the kind of activities the room supports.

Teachers are especially sensitive today to the cultural differences of the students they teach. They will be happy to know that in this area of dynamic and important differences, color is a constant. Whether students are black or white or shades of in-between, race seems not to be an important variable in color preferences. To everyone, yellow-red is the warmest of colors and green-blue the coldest. Black is the perfect dark color, and white the perfect light one. All other colors are merely lighter or darker. The preference for red and blue is universal. The shift from yellow to green is linked to age and maturity and is apparently culture-free.

Color and Behavior

Certain colors have special appeal and are related to specific behaviors. Red, for example, has more appetite appeal than any other color. Consequently red is usually found somewhere in the decor of most restaurants and on the wrappers of many food products. Red and white have probably sold more toothpaste than any other color combination. The managers of school lunch rooms should insist that red appear somewhere in the decoration of their cafeterias. Even a red band around a white serving tray might increase food consumption. Certainly some experimentation is worth the effort.

Blue, violet, and purple, on the other hand, have little or no appetite appeal. Other colors have a specialized appeal. Green, for example, will sell vegetables in the supermarket, but a green wrapper has never been known to sell bread.

There is evidence that most people behave in predictable ways when certain colors are displayed prominently in the environment. Red disturbs the equilibrium of the body, according to some authorities. It raises blood pressure and pulse rate, followed by a reversal of these symptoms. It increases restlessness and nervous tension. Insurance statistics show that red automobiles are involved in a disproportionate number of accidents. Modified forms of red, when used carefully as accenting colors, are quite beautiful and have a universal appeal. Red turns attention from within to the surrounding environment. There are numerous times and many activities during the course of the school day when students need to turn their attention outward. The intelligent use of red in the environment may encourage and support the transition from self to external events.

Green is a pacifier. This is the reason for its widespread use in schools, hospitals, and other institutions. It supports the traditional view of a school as a place where students withdraw from life and worldly stimulation to engage in study and meditation. When displayed prominently, green tends to reduce nervous tension and muscle activity.

If a teacher wants to "turn students on" and get them actively involved in the dynamics of living and in the problems of today, then a predominantly green environment is probably working against him. There are times, of course, when students ought to be reflective. The teacher must decide and attempt to support each activity with a facilitating color environment. Perhaps in the near future teachers will be able to control the color of classrooms through various color combinations of indirect lighting blended directly from consoles on their desks.

Blue is a tranquilizer. It decreases hormonal activity and lowers blood pressure and pulse rate, followed by a reversal of these effects. Blue is low in attention value and should therefore be used discriminately by the teacher. It is a restful color.

Color affects human movement. Dark colors in a room discourage people from lingering. They move faster and cover more ground, but they do not spend much time in a dark-colored room. Dark colors on the floor and upholstery of an airplane tend to give passengers a sense of security. Although Americans travel a great deal, evidently they are not completely comfortable with traveling. Advertising research shows that pictures of people boarding ships, trains, and airplanes have less readership appeal, and hence sell fewer products, than pictures of people disembarking.

Merchandisers have taken advantage of people's normal reactions to color to persuade them to buy more products. Over the past few decades the Christmas season has begun earlier and earlier. Although Christmas does not occur until December 25, "psychological Christmas" begins now in late September or early October, when merchants start decorating in red and green. Subtly they are persuading people to start purchasing earlier and to keep on purchasing until Christmas Eve. "Psychological spring" begins in the middle of January. One would imagine that the merchandisers' ultimate aim is to move their customers from one psycho-season to the next without interruption. Perhaps there are a few ideas here that teachers might use to their own advantage.

Color in Schools and Classrooms

One of the most useful discoveries a teacher will make when working with color is its relativity. A friend once asked a mathematician, "How is your wife?" The mathematician thought for a moment and then replied, "Compared to what?" Colors appear lighter or darker compared with other colors. The exact same hue will appear darker or lighter depending on the background and other colors around it. Try a simple experiment. Cut two small squares from ordinary typing paper. Place one square in the center of a larger black square, and the other in the center of a larger gray square. Notice that the white on the black square seems whiter than the white on the gray square.

When working with color, contrast is more important than hue. It is not helpful to think in terms of single colors. Colors are seen in combination with other colors. Dark walls, for example, may be made to appear lighter or darker by contrasting them with other colors. It is essential then that large display areas in the classroom be of sufficient contrast with surrounding areas to attract attention. Although a teacher may have little to say about the color of his classroom walls, he and his students have everything to say about the color and attractiveness of display areas. Through creative attractive contrasts, a teacher can make the drabbest of walls come alive.

Wall colors have a task to perform in any room. They serve as background for the people and objects in the room. Their primary mission is to enhance and facilitate the activities of the room. In a teacher's own living room, the walls are the backdrop against which he and his guests perform. They are not supposed to inhibit or detract from social gatherings. The lovelier a wallpaper is, the less fitted it is for this service. Because of its own inherent beauty, attractive wallpaper calls attention to itself and away from the host, his guests, room furniture, and the socializing process. The ideal living room color is calm and reserved, a faithful background against which objects and people look their best. It never intrudes into the foreground.

In the elementary classroom, color specialists recommend warm yellows, peach, and pink as the dominant colors. These colors are stimulating for young children, encouraging them to move about, to participate, and to express themselves. For the secondary classroom, green, blue-green, blue, and gray are recommended to avoid distraction and aid in concentration. The color specialist's view of the secondary school tends to be rather traditional.

The secondary teacher who encourages active participation by students will probably modify the latter color scheme through the addition of accent red, orange, yellow, and other warm colors in prominent display areas. It is suggested also that the colors of the room reflect and support as much as possible the activities of the room. Language laboratories, for example, where students work by themselves with relatively little interaction should be painted a moderate blue or green to reinforce the sedentary nature of the task. Where walls receive excessive sunlight, light yellows and other highly reflective surfaces should be avoided. Usually, colors in the moderate range are recommended. The interior walls of many schools are unfinished cement block. In this case, color specialists suggest finishing in gloss enamels to enhance the surface texture of the block.

The color scheme of school corridors should be light and uniform to aid in the flow of traffic. One wall of stairwells should be painted in an accent color, and the other wall in a contrasting light gray or off-white. This scheme, too, tends to facilitate the flow of traffic. The doors to fire exits should be painted an impact red or orange-red for quick and easy identification and should be uniform throughout the school. Direct illumination and light colors in rest rooms encourage cleanliness. School principals have discovered that light colors encourage the common man's art form, graffiti, especially in the men's rest rooms. Some new architectural designs call for a "graffiti wall" where visitors are encouraged to express themselves. Schools are probably not ready for this innovation yet. Perhaps the best answer is to remove the graffiti as quickly as it appears, thus discouraging further attempts. The answer is not to paint walls and doors black or dark brown. This act will present more problems than it solves in keeping rest rooms clean and tidy.

Within their own classrooms there is much that teachers can do to make the environment attractive and comfortable for themselves and their students. It is a perplexing fact that many teachers, reasonable, sensitive, and intelligent people in most respects, teach day after day in rooms and under conditions that undermine the very task they are attempting to perform. These same people know the importance of color decoration in their own homes. They understand the importance of color in their living rooms, kitchens, and bedrooms. Yet many will not lift a hand to change and enhance a classroom where they and hundreds of students spend many hours a day engaged in one of the most difficult of all human tasks, learning.

Teachers must become sensitive to the total learning environment. Surely a classroom is at least as important as a supermarket, a dentist's waiting room, or a theater lounge. Yet, these places are decorated in such a way that they support and facilitate specific kinds of activity. Classrooms deserve at least the same attention. Decorate, display, make the room an exciting place to be in. Challenge the eye to inspect, to wonder, to frame questions, and seek answers. Turn old closets and shelves into places where students can browse and learn at ease and in comfort.

If classroom shelving is utilized for display areas, a few suggestions offered by retail merchandisers may help. The shelves themselves ought to be spotless and sagless. Paint-streaked, sagging shelves, covered with soiled paper and riddled with nail and thumbtack holes speak eloquently to students of the unimportance of the display. A teacher's lack of concern will be repaid by students' lack of attention. Paint shelves in pastel colors.

If possible, vary their height and width to form pleasing, interesting patterns.

The objects in the display should not be shown flat if they can be arranged otherwise. Use white space between related groups of objects. White edits color. It partitions and divides the total display into a logical series of related parts and ties the parts together to form an attractive whole. White serves the same function on posters, bulletin boards, and other display spaces. White is such a strong boundary that with only a thin white line between them, red may be run into pink and still create a pleasing effect.

Color and Personality

Although a person may believe that he chooses his own colors, there are psychologists who have amassed considerable evidence that colors choose him! Choice, in other words, is not free but is forced on one by physical and psychological factors beyond one's control. There is nothing very mysterious about this. If, for example, a person has experienced an emotionally tumultuous period recently in his life, or if he tends to be the sort of person without great reserves of energy, then he may seek colors that require little energy to look at. On the other hand, if he possesses unusual reserves of energy, he will tend to seek colors that tap this hidden reservoir. In seeking some colors and rejecting others, a person communicates some basic needs, and by determining these needs, psychologists are able to make inferences about his personality. When a teacher adjusts his color television receiver, for example, he may make important non-verbal statements about himself. If he heightens the reds, he tends to be self-confident and full of physical vitality. If he mutes them, on the other hand, he may be a self-effacing person. If he intensifies the blues, he is probably a passive soul who enjoys peace and quiet. If he is inclined to be a chronic optimist, he may turn up the yellow. And if he finds himself enjoying heightened violet, he might tend to be a bit neurotic.

Psychological color testing has grown quite sophisticated over the past one or two decades. Although they are not too popular in the United States, color tests are used throughout Europe by psychologists, physicians, and industry. These tests have the decided advantage of being nonverbal, hence there is no vocabulary problem. Also they are relatively culture-free since color belongs to everyone; it is a universal language.

To give some idea of how color testing works, try this just-for-fun version. From the colors listed below, select the color you prefer most and the color you prefer least. Remember, do not choose the colors that look well on you. Sometimes the colors we like best, we cannot wear. Cover the right side of the pages, choose the ones you *prefer most* and *least* from the list of colors below, and then check the remarks under the appropriate heading.

	Prefer Most	*Prefer Least*
Red	You are strong-willed, tend to be impulsive, and seek an active, adventuresome life. Do you sometimes exaggerate and over-dramatize?	Things may not be going well for you. You feel out of sorts and probably need a rest. You tend to be irritable. If you selected blue as your most preferred color, frustrations and anxieties are getting the best of you.

Yellow	You want to be important and to be held in high regard by others. You are hoping for happiness and release from past problems. You have great faith in the future.	You have been disappointed and you may feel empty inside. You have given up hope—therefore you may be suspicious and mistrusting of others.
Blue	You want a calm, orderly life with no surprises and no complex involvements. You have integrity and you expect others to have integrity. You trust others and you want to be trusted.	You find your current status burdensome. You may be agitated and restless, eager to escape. You find it hard to concentrate while in this condition. Would you like to just run away from it all?
Violet	You have a great deal of charm and fascination. You appreciate the finer things, but you tend to be a bit irresponsible. If you are a woman, you may also be pregnant. There is evidence that pregnant women have a high preference for violet.	You may have turned away from people and now lavish your attention on objects of a scientific artistic nature. You are reserved in human relationships until you know exactly what is expected of you.
Green	You are opinionated and a great talker. You are the "reformer-type"—better life, better health, better everything for everybody.	You need recognition but you may not be getting it. You may have turned sour on the world and have become bitter and sarcastic.
Black	You are a rebel—you want to topple everything. But be careful, because you often act unwisely and this could lead to your downfall.	You have a normal tendency to hang on to what you want and to control your own destiny.

Brown   You like to be comfortable—good food, good
drink, nice easy chair.
Contentment is very im-
portant to you.

You think you are made
of stern stuff. You don't
need comfort; you are a
rugged individualist.

Gray   You are a middle-of-the
roader, unwilling to com-
mit yourself to anything.
You don't believe in get-
ting involved.

You may be meddlesome
and perhaps a little in-
trusive. You would like
to have your hand in
everything going on
around you.

The Luminous Environment

Any discussion of color would not be complete without
touching upon the importance of a properly well lighted
classroom. Most classrooms are adequate in this respect,
but there are instances of flagrant violations. When
schools become overcrowded, classrooms are sometimes
set up in gyms, lunchrooms, temporary buildings, or
other spaces that will accommodate a teacher and a number of students.

The teacher has an obligation to speak out when ex-
pediency takes precedence over maintaining a healthy
learning environment. Fatigue rates rise in direct proportion to the dimming of the visual field. This is a
fact, plain and simple. So much of a student's work depends on visual scanning and identification that lowered
light levels will decrease his efficiency drastically,
thereby decreasing the quality and quantity of his work.

The human eye is most comfortable when there are
no great contrasts in the visual field. This does not mean
that everything must be of uniform brightness. Simply
avoid large areas of dark and light. Ordinarily this will

pose few problems. However, temporary classrooms in hallways, auditoriums or other areas where there may be drastic changes in light levels will distract and fatigue students.

There are three simple rules of illumination that will assist teachers in controlling the luminous environment:

1. Maintain high levels of illumination. Everything else being equal, the higher the light level, the less strain on the eyes. When students must expend energy just seeing, there is less energy left to understand what is being seen.

2. All areas of the room should be balanced in brightness. And this is important—the brightest part of the room, ideally, should be in the immediate vicinity of students' work areas. Factory and assembly line workers have their work well illuminated. Industry has known for a long time that eye fatigue plays havoc with production schedules. Yet school authorities sometimes ignore this obvious fact. To avoid sharp contrasts the visual field around the task, ideally, should be only one-third as bright as the work area. Lastly, no part of the visual field should be brighter than the immediate vicinity of the task.

3. Avoid glare either from direct light sources or from reflecting surfaces.

Without color the world would certainly be a drab and dreary place. Yet color does more than decorate. It is part of an individual's microspace that shapes him and which he manipulates to reach a better accommodation with his own environment. Color is a silent language, a unique and subtle symbol system used by humans, consciously and subconsciously, to send each other information. Teachers who try to understand this language and use it creatively and intelligently will help their students to be more productive.

FOR FURTHER READING

Baker, Stephen. *Visual Persuasion*. New York: McGraw-Hill, 1961.

Birren, Faber. *Color: A Survey in Words and Pictures*. New York: University Books, 1963.

Child, Irving L., et al. "Age & Sex Differences in Children's Color Preferences." *Child Development*, vol. 39, no. 1, March 1968, pp. 237–47.

Fitch, James Marston. "Control of the Luminous Environment." *Scientific American*, Sept. 1968, pp. 191–214.

Gregory, Richard L. "Visual Illusions." *Scientific American*, Nov. 1968, pp. 66–76.

Identification of Colors for Building. Washington, D.C.: Building Research Institute, Inc., Report No. BRI-PUB-1001, 1961.

Kleeman, Walter Jr. *Some New Bases and Needs for Interior Design From Environmental Research*. New York: The NSID Interior Environment Research Council, 1968.

Luscher, Max. *The Luscher Color Test*, trans. and ed. by Ian A. Scott. New York: Random House, 1969.

Manger, Emily M. *Modern Display Techniques*. New York: Fairchild, 1964.

Mueller, Conrad, and Rudolph, Mae. *Light and Vision*. New York: Time-Life Books, 1966.

Reuner, Paul. *Color Order and Harmony*. New York: Reinhold, 1964.

Scrivestava, Rajendra N. *Human Movement as a Function of Color Stimulation*. Topeka, Kan.: Environmental Research Foundation, 1968.

Wright, W. D. *The Rays Are Not Colored*. New York: American Elsevier, 1968.

THE LANGUAGE
OF FACES

For centuries poets, painters, and song writers have attempted to capture the meaning and mystery of the human face. Until fairly recently they had few competitors. These artists drew attention to the shape and features of the face. They pointed to the eyes, the beautiful, mysterious human eyes, and through them permitted people to glimpse universal emotions. They showed the human mouth smiling with contentment or compressed in resignation. They declared to the world, this face is noble, this face is depraved, this is a proud face, and here is the face of innocence.

Theoreticians may write and speak about learning in the abstract, as though it existed as a disembodied bio-chemical process, but a good teacher knows that learning is a personal experience. Each student in a teacher's class learns individually and alone, and whether a teacher realizes it or not, many of the inferences and assumptions he makes regarding the learning process of his students are based on information gained by reading faces. Unfortunately, sometimes his information may be incorrect or incomplete. Intuition, even artistic intuition, is incapable of supplying consistently reliable data.

Since midcentury, however, the face has begun to reveal some of its secrets to persistent researchers. Do people communicate with their faces? Yes indeed. Are people aware of the facial messages they are transmitting? Sometimes they are, but frequently they are not. Do people, then, have little conscious control over some kinds of facial movement and expression? Apparently that is the case in many instances. Even such a simple expression as a smile is a complex pattern of muscle movements, which may involve muscles of the scalp and neck as well as the face. No one could begin to monitor and control such complex movements. How many different facial expressions can a person make, and does each expression have a meaning? The answer to the first part of the question is thousands; the answer to the second requires some elaboration.

Consider, for example, a fairly common facial expression—the wink. What does a wink mean? A wink could be described somatically in terms of the interplay of certain muscles. But, you say, what does a wink *mean?* Well, obviously, the meaning you have in mind is social, that is, when one person winks at another person, what is he saying, nonverbally? Now interpretations become complicated. Before that question can be answered, other prior questions must be answered. Who winked at whom? When? Where? How? What words were spoken? What was the rest of the winker's body doing? When these questions have been answered, the meaning of a wink might become clear.

In other words, the meaning of specific body movements, including facial expressions, cannot usually be determined outside social frames of reference. This is the view of some leading authorities in the field. To state the meaning of a wink, therefore, one must know the complete social context of which the wink is merely one single component.

There is another minority point of view that presents evidence that some human facial expressions are universal and not related specifically to one culture or another. A happy smile on the face of a Peruvian Indian is identified as expressing feelings of joy by other people in other cultures all over the world. All people, everywhere, use their faces to express basic human emotions in essentially the same way.

Now there is a fundamental difference between these two points of view that must be recognized if the material in this chapter and those that follow is to be interpreted objectively. If facial expressions are culture-based, they are learned and will vary significantly from culture to culture. If, on the other hand, facial expressions are universal, they are "wired-in" genetically to every human being. In this view faces are "programmed" to behave a certain way when certain events occur in the environment. If this is so, there will be little significant variation in the meaning of specific facial expressions or body movements among people of different cultures.

Which view is correct? Probably both. It is not surprising that Freudian analysts keep finding people who have Freudian dreams. Nor is it surprising that sociologists, anthropologists, and workers in related social fields are able to rationalize and support a social base for their findings in nonverbal communication. There can be no doubt about it—a significant social dimension to nonverbal communication does exist—but if past experience is a reliable guide, there are other important dimensions yet to be uncovered. As researchers with different backgrounds explore the field, other points of view may be expected to shape our thinking.

From either point of view, however, and based on reliable evidence, teachers may assume that most movements of the human body, including the face, have meaning. Body motions and expressions are not usually random. They are logical patterns of behavior, and, being logical, they are subject to analyses. The validity of the analyses, of course, will depend on the expertise of the investigators and the experiments on which they base their data. The human body does speak a language of its own and will yield information to anyone who understands the language.

Anthropologists and sociologists make some further assumptions that should to be kept in mind as their data are considered. They assume that since human beings live in communities, visible body movements and expressions are communicative acts taught by the community to the individual so that the community may influence the behavior of the individual, and the individual, in turn, may influence the behavior of the community. Each individual within the community is permitted some small personal variation in behavior, but even their minor idiosyncracies may be considered within the general framework of the larger social system.

Certainly there is sufficient evidence on hand to support the above assumptions. As noted in previous chapters, even the way an individual utilizes the space around him seems to be culture-oriented. Culture is a significant variable in any study of nonverbal languages, and it is extremely risky at present to generalize body movement and expression beyond the particular culture that yields the supporting data.

Nonverbal communication in its many and varied forms has in recent years been the subject of numerous popular books and magazine articles. These publications are usually intended for popular consumption and serve a useful purpose in keeping the general public abreast of a new and interesting field of study. The teacher should approach them with caution, however. They are not intended and should not be used to provide professional guidelines for teachers. In fact, they have been largely responsible for a kind of mythology that has grown up around nonverbal communication because they present a rather simplistic view of human behavior. Teachers should know that human behavior is extremely complex, much of it beyond understanding at the moment. Thus at the outset of this discussion of body movement and expression, some basic premises and limitations of the data must be kept in mind.

Particular gestures and movements have little meaning in and of themselves. They yield meaning only as the larger pattern of behavior of which they are a part is identified and understood. For example, although it has been stated that female hair-twirling is associated with emotional immaturity, this does not mean that every girl who twirls her hair is emotionally immature. It simply means that hair-twirling could be part of a larger pattern which, if identified, might provide evidence to support the original hypothesis.

Nor is one particular component of a pattern more significant than any other component. Hair-twirling, once again, is not the most significant element in a pattern of behavior associated with emotional immaturity in girls. Unless there is evidence to the contrary, each element is as significant as every other element, and all must be given equal weight. Since it is not known how many and what kind of elements comprise entire behavior patterns, teachers must be careful not to jump to hasty conclusions.

Nonverbal languages cannot be considered apart from verbal language. When one person communicates with another, his words, gestures, and facial expressions together comprise an array of information that must be considered in its totality. The meaning of the communication is not in the words alone, nor in the gestures alone, nor in facial expressions alone. Each kind of language adds a unique dimension to the message. All contribute to meaning, especially when body language apparently seems to contradict verbal language.

Body language is not primitive in the sense that it is a vestigial remnant of a mode of communication that predated words. Indeed, the movements and expressions of the body are sometimes more sophisticated than the words people use. Notice the way teachers use their own bodies to help students understand concepts that are difficult to convey by words alone. Have you ever tried to describe a spiral staircase to someone using words alone?

Body language is not a modifier of verbal language. It is a mode of communication in its own right. Researchers assume that it is logical, patterned, and predictable. When human beings wish to pass information to each other, body language is a primary channel of communication.

Since the body has many parts, each of which is capable of some degree of independent motion and expression, the body itself is a composite of many sublanguages. The trunk, limbs, head, eyes, mouth—all speak a dialect of their own. For the purpose of analysis it is often permissable to isolate each part and study it individually. It must be remembered, however, that the real, actual meaning of body communication may be derived only through observing and identifying the totality, the complete pattern, of communication, including the verbal.

Eyes

When a teacher meets a student for the first time, his eyes are immediately drawn to the student's face. Depending on his interest, he may examine the face rather casually or quite carefully. (The student, by the way, is engrossed in the same task.) The first brief encounter with the eyes is a significant moment in this intense dialogue.

Look steadily into the pupils of the eyes. Do you feel comfortable? Do you feel the other person is interested in you? Do you like him? Note the size of the pupils. If you are a careful observer and if the level of illumination is sufficient, you may witness a startling phenomenon. The size of the pupils may grow larger or smaller even as you look at them.

Just a few years ago it was believed that the size of the pupils of the eyes held constant if the level of illumination remained constant. Since then, however, sufficient evidence has been collected to demonstrate that the pupils of the eyes respond to events in the environment in a predictable way. They open wider to see things that are pleasant and agreeable and close down noticeably at the sight of disagreeable people, objects, and events. The size of the pupils is a reliable indicator of a person's attitude toward people and events in his environment.

Strangely enough, the eyes respond not only to visual events in the environment but also to sounds. Therefore in a teacher's first brief encounter with a new student, the sound of his voice may also affect the student's eyes. Under laboratory conditions the eyes of subjects have been photographed on motion picture film. Later when the enlarged image was projected on a screen, the changing size of the pupils was readily seen. In real life, however, unless the other person reacts strongly, one may experience difficulty detecting any change in the size of the pupils. But if a teacher keeps watching, sooner or later his patience will surely be rewarded.

Subconsciously, through the eyes, a person tells other people what he thinks of them. Subconsciously, other people receive the messages and respond. For example, if a student approaches a teacher, speaks to him, perhaps touches him, the teacher's eyes respond. Naturally the student may not consciously be aware of the changing size of the pupils. Subconsciously, however, he may receive the message that the teacher accepts, rejects, or is indifferent toward him. If a teacher's words happen to contradict what is seen in his face, the student will believe the teacher's face, not his words. Consequently, and sometimes to a teacher's grief and embarrassment, his eyes insist on telling the truth while his mouth is busy fibbing.

The more a person likes someone or something, the

more he looks. That certainly should not surprise teachers. Chances are, they will look more at students they like than at students they do not like. Again, this subtle message is eventually understood by students, especially by those about whom a teacher feels strongly. Looking, however, does not give a teacher license to stare.

Perhaps this is a good time to remind teachers that there are some important restrictions on staring in American culture. Once a teacher becomes interested in "eye reading," he may find himself staring intently at people. If the people are his friends, he may get away with it. Strangers are another matter. Americans are permitted by culture to stare at strangers for approximately one second. If a teacher stares longer, the stranger-student will become painfully aware of his stare. He may grow uncomfortable and embarrassed; he could react in unpredictable ways.

When strangers approach each other from a distance, they may stare as much as they wish until both are about eight feet apart. At that distance American culture dictates that they drop their eyes and not look again until each has passed. In other cultures one may stare longer. American women in Arab countries sometimes resent the long, curious stares of Arab men—but Arab culture permits prolonged scrutiny.

Civil rights demonstrators are instructed to maintain eye contact with their adversaries during confrontations. In this way they manage to preserve dignity and force others to acknowledge their humanity in many awkward, tension-loaded situations. Teachers might try imitating them. They should look at the people who are part of their lives. They should look at all their students, their fellow-workers, supervisors, and friends. They should look at everybody and force their way into the consciousness of people. They should insist that they be acknowledged as persons. They may note a pleasant change in people's attitudes toward them.

It is not by accident that when viewing photographs people tend to focus on the eyes more than on any other part of the face. Human eyes are like magnets that draw other human eyes. Little children (and adults, sometimes) cover their eyes when they believe they have done something foolish or embarrassing. This is their way of becoming invisible. By obscuring the eyes with dark glasses, some people believe they are more secure. They feel protected; they can stare without being seen. The reverse, of course, is also true. To other people, the wearer of dark glasses is always staring at them.

Just by diverting his gaze, a teacher may placate a student who is annoyed or angry with him. Students have learned this trick. Their glance to the side or downward says, "You win. I do not wish to press the issue." Other animals such as deer, elk, gulls, and gorillas use the same form of placatory gesture. When a teacher scolds a student and the student diverts his gaze, the teacher has made his point. If he is at all perceptive, he will not belabor the issue.

Probably the most effective "put down" in the world is a cold, hard stare, frequently a teacher's secret weapon. Teachers are permitted a short, one-second stare at anyone, but once they exceed their allotted time, students begin to feel less human. A person acknowledges the presence and humanity of people by looking at them and then quickly dropping his gaze before it becomes a stare. Even people seeking the public spotlight soon grow tired of being stared at. A prolonged stare is almost an invasion of privacy. The victim feels painfully visible.

Frequently someone with an unusual physical characteristic—an outlandish hair style or an exceptionally handsome face, for example—may entice a person to stare longer than he should. If his stare remains unnoticed, he may continue his furtive examination. If suddenly the other person catches him and meets his eyes with his own, he is supposed to look away first. This is a way of saying, "Sorry. I didn't mean to stare." All is forgiven, unless the other person catches him a second time or unless he fails to drop his gaze first.

A teacher's eyes are potent weapons in the classroom. His students are ever aware of them as they go about their business. His eyes can project security, trust, and tolerance, or simply by prolonged stares, he can make his students feel like objects, freaks, or non-persons who are not even permitted the small social amenity of not being scrutinized continuously. Even a physician may not stare at his patients indiscriminately. He is permitted a short "moral looking time" in which to examine eyes, face, abdomen, legs, and other body parts. If he exceeds his allotted time, both doctor and patient may grow tense. The teacher, too, must observe this "moral looking time" limit. Tense, anxious students cannot perform at their best, especially under intense scrutiny.

The Utility of Looking

No one need remind human beings of their eyes' utility. Eyes are probably the most versatile and efficient data-gathering devices found in nature. Without them humans would experience sensory deprivation beyond imagination. Besides seeing, eyes perform some other marvelous functions that are only now beginning to be appreciated.

The next time you thread your way through a crowded airport terminal or along a subway or bus platform during rush hour, notice how infrequently people collide. Ordinarily the random movement of so many people in so many different directions would be expected, statistically, to produce frequent collisions. Yet collisions are so rare that when they do occur, they catch people by surprise and they apologize, or are apologized to, profusely. How does one manage to move through a crowd with such precision?

Earlier it was noted that people are permitted by culture to look at individuals until they are approximately eight feet away. Then they must divert their gaze. But before they do, they signal to the other person by means of a fleeting glance in the proper direction whether they are going to pass on the right or left of him. The other person signals back, and each passes the other safely and smoothly. When collisions occur, either one person signalled that he would pass in one direction, changed his mind, and attempted to pass in the other or either or both persons failed to send or receive the customary eye signals.

These "passing" glances are but one of many routine chores human eyes perform. Normal conversation, for example, would be a confusing experience indeed were it not for the eyes. Normally, when a person first begins to speak to someone, he looks away. This is his signal to the other person that he intends to keep the floor for a while. Since he must pause occasionally for breath or to arrange his thoughts, he signals to his partner that he is not quite finished by glancing away during these pauses. This glance off to the side means, "I am not finished yet. Do not interrupt me." His partner will usually respect the rules of this little game. He knows that when the first person is finished, he will pause and look directly at him. This is his cue to take over. People who do not observe the rules of conversation and who frequently interrupt are annoying because they circumvent established social procedure. By their behavior they inform others that they are not important enough to be granted the usual social courtesies. Thus, if a teacher happens to be a chronic interrupter, his students will not excuse him. Everyone, regardless of age, is entitled to the floor until the customary signals are exchanged and acknowledged.

Sometimes when conversing with friends or colleagues, a teacher may not agree with what they are saying. He signals his disagreement, or at least his reluctance to agree completely, by glancing away while they are speaking. When colleagues notice this, they may elaborate further or go into detail to explain themselves. If a person looks directly at someone while he is speaking, this is his way of saying, "Listen to me. I know what I am talking about." If, at the same time, the other person looks away—well, of such stuff are arguments made.

In small group discussions, or for that matter during afternoon bridge games or backyard barbecues, it is usually easy to recognize the dominant personality. He is the fellow who is always looking away when someone else is talking. If two people within the group hold dissimilar views, they may direct prolonged but infrequent looks at each other as they speak. These long looks between opponents probably represent a search for cues that signal acceptance of a particular point of view.

In every group there are people who like to talk and others who would rather listen. One will usually find the listeners looking frequently at the speaker. And the talkers? They are the ones who look away the most. Wouldn't it be helpful if somehow we could educate students to take advantage of the best characteristics of both—fluent talkers who are also looking listeners?

If a teacher has not paid much attention to the way people look and do not look at each other, perhaps he now realizes that he is missing important information. With some discipline and practice, he may become a skilled observer of human behavior. Here are just a few generalizations he may be able to verify from his own experience.

1. People who get along well together look at each other frequently in friendly, social situations. If these same people are placed in a competitive situation, they will look at each other less frequently.
2. Autistic children (and schizophrenic adults) seldom look at anyone.
3. People who excel in abstract thinking, such as philosophy tend to look more than people who excel in concrete thinking such as electronics.
4. Whenever a personal topic is introduced into a group conversation, people look at each other less frequently.
5. As a general rule, women look at people more than men. Women are avid "lookers," hence they see

more. (Could this account in part for women's so called "intuition"?)

In American culture people are expected to look others directly in the eye when matters of personal integrity are discussed. Americans are naturally suspicious of "shifty-eyed" individuals. Apparently there is some validity to these long-held hunches. An honest man will usually drop his gaze when confronted with evidence of his own dishonesty. If this always happened, perhaps life would not be so complicated for teachers who must sometimes make decisions concerning the honesty of others.

Occasionally one may run into a "Machiavellian" personality-type. He may be the earnest young man (or woman) who looks a person straight in the eye and in a forthright manner tells some of the biggest fibs. He is cunning, and he has mastered all the signs and signals of honesty, which he uses to serve his own ends. He is no particular age; he may be six or sixty. He has no particular occupation; he may be a student in a teacher's class or the neighbor next door. In short, he is a "con man." He is difficult to recognize. Should he be accused of wrongdoing to his face, he will undoubtedly convince the accuser with his honest gaze that he has made a terrible mistake. The accuser may even apologize to him for ever doubting his integrity.

Lookers—Left and Right

An intriguing notion frequently alluded to in the arts but without much scientific basis regards the eyes as a projection of personality. What, really, can one tell about a person by looking at his eyes? Recently a series of interesting studies hold promise of a remarkably rich field of data.

Previously it was noted that during the course of a conversation both the person who is talking and the person who is listening frequently glance off to the side. These are conversational cues that tell a person when he may enter a conversation and whether his argument is being received favorably by the listener. One looks off to the side to think and to avoid the distraction of the other person's face. If someone were to ask a question that involved some conscious manipulation of ideas or numbers, before answering the person would probably glance sidewards. This joint movement of the eyes to the left or right is called a CLEM—conjugate-lateral eye movement.

CLEMs are not made randomly to the left or right. Most people tend to glance most of the time in one direction or the other. One is either a left-looker or a right-looker. In attempting to account for this prefer- ence for the left or right, researchers have related CLEMs to the dominance of left or right cerebral hemi- spheres. People who glance frequently to the left are believed to possess a dominant right hemisphere, and *vice versa*. As a precautionary note, some authorities at present agree that dominance appears to shift from one hemisphere to the other depending on the behavior under observation and the function the brain happens to be performing at the moment. After all, both hemi- spheres are connected. But in general, there is strong evidence that one hemisphere frequently appears to dominate certain behaviors. Unfortunately, these studies seem to apply only to males. Females seem to look to left or right without any apparent pattern.

Males who glance off to the left while thinking tend to excel in the creation of vivid imagery and in non-verbal functions. They are emotionally subjective, relax better during stress, and are good at synthesizing ideas. They are more sociable than right-lookers, more creative, and score higher on the verbal and writing portions of scholastic aptitude scales. Usually left-lookers regard themselves as more religious and more musically talented than most people.

Right-lookers, on the other hand, excel in analytical thinking and usually score higher on quantitative test scales. They can do with less sleep and seem to make their career choices earlier. They tend to tense-up during stress situations, pay more attention to the right side of their bodies, and prefer cool colors. As a general rule, left-lookers tend to seek careers in the classical/humanist areas and right-lookers in the quantitative/science areas.

Each part of the face capable of some movement and expression may be utilized for communication. Eyelids, for example open and close. Admittedly, that isn't much, but even this simple behavior yields information. Men are expected to close and open their eyelids in one continuous movement. Should they keep their eyelids closed even for a fraction of time, they are signalling either drowsiness or distress. Women, however, are permitted a wider latitude of eyelid behavior. They may close their eyes and open them without a perceptible duration of holding. They may close and hold for a fraction of a second. They may close slowly and open immediately. Or they may close slowly and hold. Each pattern accompanies a particular type of verbal message.

Twenty-three different positions of the eyebrows have been identified. Men are more versatile than women in utilizing the message-sending capabilities of the eyebrows. Even the absence of eyebrows provides information. Can you imagine the subtle change in the expression of the Mona Lisa if da Vinci had chosen to give her eyebrows? Just by raising the eyebrows a man can ask a question. By lowering them he may express confusion and doubt. By raising one eyebrow and lowering the other, he may express skepticism.

The language of human eyes is eloquent. When a teacher scolds a student or embarrasses him, he may look away. He is telling the teacher silently but insistently, "Can't you see you do not exist? I have sent you away; I can no longer see you." And what could be more eloquent than human tears? Why do humans cry? No one seems to know. The best guess is that tears are a unique human plea for assistance. Tears are distressing to other humans. Evidently the real meaning of tears is understood by all humans but at a subconscious level.

Smile!

One of the first facial expressions human beings learn to make is the smile. Smiling has long been associated with joy and contentment, yet the most reliable clues available point to very different origins.

According to recent theories, the smile is a direct descendant of the grin, and the grin had two origins. The grin began as a protective behavior, the baring of the teeth as a preliminary act to biting or spitting out.

Many mammals grin when startled. The Rhesus monkey, for example, frequently grins to itself when it is startled. So does the oppossum. And so do people! If a heavy door slips from a person's grasp and he knows that it is going to slam shut with a bang, he may find himself standing there, helpless, gritting his teeth waiting for the inevitable to happen. If a person drives a "stick-shift" car, he probably grins when he grinds the gears. People, Rhesus monkeys, and oppossums share this common primitive behavior—they bare their teeth in preparation for attacking or being attacked by something unpleasant.

The second origin of the grin was to support the muscles of the neck during high pitched vocalization such as screaming. Originally the grin was accompanied by a growl, snarl, or scream. In humans the scream has disappeared, although some kind of sound may accompany a human grin. Usually the grin represents both the readiness to bite and to scream.

From the grin and the scream came the smile and vocal laughter. But a profound mystery is evident. How did these primitive expressions ever become associated with pleasure?

It may have happened this way. Zoologists have noted that in some advanced types of primates such as the baboon, the grin is used as a defensive gesture showing good intentions. A male baboon may approach another strange male, grinning, to signify that although he is ready to defend himself, his intentions are good. When a person is introduced to a stranger, does he not shake hands and smile?

There is much evidence to show that humans seek a continually changing sensory environment. They become bored with the familiar; they seek out the new and the startling. The primitive response to startling stimuli was baring the teeth in preparation for attack. Thus humans seek out the new that is pleasurable, but somewhere in the dark recesses of their brain an alarm is sounded. They go on the defensive. They shake hands and grin.

Infants are startled out of their wits when a parent peeps around a door and says, "Boo!" But they laugh and want more. Surprise is the essence of all adult humor. Originally surprise meant attack, but through the ages, at least for humans, most startling stimuli turned out to be pleasurable. Hence they seek the new and the startling, but when it happens, they bare their teeth in a grin.

To understand the smile one must understand something about the social context in which it occurs. If a person has traveled extensively throughout the United States and is an alert observer, he may have noticed that people smile more in the South than in the North or Midwest. One may smile at strangers in Mobile or Atlanta without too many people interpreting the smile for more than it is, a friendly greeting between two human beings. But if one smiles at strangers in Philadelphia or Indianapolis, one may have gone beyond the bounds of acceptable behavior among strangers. Strangers do not readily smile at each other in the North. A southern girl working in a northern city soon learns to smile less or invite unwelcome consequences. So a smile is not always just a smile. Where one smiles and at whom one smiles are also important.

Teachers may notice that students sometimes smile

as a form of apology. If a teacher catches a student doing something he ought not to be doing—cheating during a test, for example—he may smile. Do not misunderstand these kinds of smiles. They are not really smiles. The student is not laughing at the teacher. He has been caught red-handed, and he is baring his teeth in the primitive, defensive response. If he could verbalize his subconscious feelings he might say, "You have caught me! This is an unpleasant situation. I am embarrassed." If a teacher finds himself in this sort of situation, he should not belabor the point. He should never say, "Wipe that silly grin off your face!" It is not a grin. It is a primitive snarl that evolution has silenced. A humane teacher will retire and permit the student to recover.

The contented little smiles of new-born babies are often a source of wonderment to new parents. Folklore has attributed these smiles to gas, and this myth has been handed down from mother to daughter for ages. Recent findings offer another explanation.

In a study of 300 babies, two different kinds of smiles were identified. During the first two weeks of life babies smile, usually in their sleep, due to the growth of the brain stem. The brain stem is one of the more primitive portions of the brain. After three weeks these sleepy smiles may continue, but now a new kind of smile appears—the social smile. The comforting sights, sounds, smells, and touches of familiar people and objects elicit the smile that brings new daddies rushing home from the office. Now begins the long process of learning which smile is used for which occasion. By the time a youngster enters first grade, he possesses an almost complete repertory of smiles.

At the present time five different kinds of human smiles have been identified. Each one or variations of it may be used on many different occasions. Although the meaning of each is not entirely clear, these five smiles may be described as follows:

Simple smile—When people are pleased with themselves and things are going well, they may smile to themselves. The lips curl back and up, and the teeth do not show.

Broad smile—This is the genuine, happy smile that accompanies pleasurable excitement. The mouth is open, lips curled back, and both upper and lower teeth are usually visible.

Lip-in smile—This smile is easily identified by the position of the lower lip, which is drawn in slightly between the teeth. It might be called the "coy girl" smile, and it usually implies subordination to the person at whom the smile is directed.

Upper smile—This is the "How do you do?" smile, the greeting one reserves for friends. It tends to linger on the face when greeting a member of one's family. It is called the "upper" smile because only the upper teeth are uncovered. The mouth is just slightly open.

Oblong smile—When is a smile not a smile? When it is an oblong smile, a fake smile. The lips are drawn fully back from the upper and lower teeth forming an oblong. This is the smile people reserve for jokes that aren't really funny and for people they wish to impress.

The human lips, aside from smiling, also perform some other functions that have communicative value. For example, people tend to compress their lips when they toy mentally with problems or ideas. Japanese fortune tellers study facial expressions, including the natural shape and texture of the lips, for clues to a person's personality and fortune. They have agreed, based on long experience, that people who purse their lips frequently have much self-control and can make quick decisions. A large mouth in men may signify unbridled ambition; in women a large mouth usually means sensuality. On the other hand, a small mouth in both men and women may indicate a rather conservative nature and a possible lack of ambition.

People with thin lips are usually intelligent. They recognize their own shortcomings. Frequently, to hide a lack of self-confidence, they may be quite talkative. Thick lips imply a cheerful, sensitive nature, although in the extreme they might also denote a slowness of intellect. People whose lips are usually parted are impatient and forgetful. They experience difficulty in completing things.

Among the Japanese, dark lips are associated with bad luck, family trouble, and unhappiness in love. And of course natural, red lips signify a happy family life and good fortune. Lips that curl slightly upward at the corners belong to people who are cheerful and well liked. If they curl up in the extreme, however, they could also denote arrogance and extravagance. Lips that curl downward belong to the "sufferers," the people who always seem to struggle against formidable odds.

Fortune-telling through lip reading is fun but cannot be taken seriously. Experience cannot substitute for evidence. The Japanese, however, have recently pushed their concepts a little further. Their interest in lip reading has led to "lip prints," the imprints formed by the groove of the lips. According to their evidence, no two human lip prints are alike. Hence lip prints are a reliable form of identification which, like finger prints, have already been admitted as evidence in Japanese courts of law.

Facial Expression

In American culture, although people may cover certain parts of their bodies at times and are required by law to cover other parts at all times, the face has usually been free of regulation. Faces usually are uncovered. Consequently Americans are face-conscious. Unlike the so-called "inscrutible" faces of Orientals or the covered faces of Arab women, American faces have been permitted by culture to express feelings openly. In fact, in daily interaction people search the faces of other people for clues to their attitudes and feelings.

Physiologists have estimated that the musculature of the human face makes possible more than 20,000 different facial expressions! Of these at the present time a scant twenty-six or so have been identified and described. But researchers are on the threshold of a brand new source of information about people, which should prove to be of immense value in the future.

Contrary to what one might think, it is extremely difficult for a number of reasons to study the animated human face. Expressions occur as responses to internal and external sets of conditions. Since a laboratory is limited in the number and kind of conditions it can support, a laboratory setting is a pale, one dimensional substitute for the richness and variety of real life. Therefore, it is difficult to generalize from the laboratory to life situations. Also, the speed at which people signal each other is phenomenal. For example, micro-expressions, fleeting fragments of head, eye, mouth, and eyelid movements streak by at about one-twentieth of a second. Even if a researcher has been fortunate enough to evoke and record such expressions on film or videotape, he may not notice them during playback. Perhaps the analysis of human facial expression is a job for the computer.

To understand the meaning of facial expressions some researchers have attempted to trace them back to their primitive beginnings. The great Charles Darwin was among the first to undertake this difficult task. More recently, anthropologists and zoologists have pushed back the frontiers of knowledge in this little-known area, advancing educated guesses, hunches, and hypotheses that are beginning to shed some light on man's origins. Some of their theories are intriguing.

Unlike rain forest primates, which can scurry up trees at the approach of threatening intruders, plains monkeys must rely on cunning and group cooperation. Plains chimpanzees organize for an attack. They have been observed running upright to do battle, swinging clubs over their shoulders and encouraging each other with embraces and handshakes.

Evidently, then, the plains habitat of our human ancestors demanded sets of skills and competencies unneeded by many other animals for survival. A high premium was placed on communication within the group, an economy of expression that could convey important information instantly and accurately. The reason, of course, was for protection, to promote cooperation, and to reduce inter-group conflict. It has generally been acknowledged that the plains habitat may have promoted hunting and the use of tools. At present there is speculation that the plains may also have been the breeding ground, the primordial "social soup," out of which came smiling, laughter, and language.

Human facial expressions may have had their origins in the "togetherness" of the open plains. The possible origin of the human smile, a once functional behavior that has survived because of its communicative value, has already been discussed. Similarly, the human frown probably arose from staring at close objects. Dogs, capuchin monkeys, and other animals with mobile faces lower their eyebrows. The gesture may have been to aid focusing the eyes or as a form of protection for the eyes.

The direct stare in most mammals is a fairly valid indication of concentrated effort and little or no fear. The fixed stare with lowered brow often precedes attack. It has become an expression of confident threat in monkeys, apes, and humans. Teachers may notice this expression on the faces of student who "stand up" to authority figures. It means, "I am not afraid of you."

Most of the information available at present is fragmentary. Much of it has been collected under laboratory conditions by asking people to express specific emotions on their faces, then asking other people to identify the emotions, or by asking subjects to identify facial emotions depicted on sets of drawings or photographs. The literature in this area is extensive and goes back many decades. Happiness seems to be the easiest facial expression to read. Other emotions are more difficult to identify. In one typical experiment happiness was correctly identified seventy percent of the time. Contempt, on the other hand, was correctly identified only thirty-three percent of the time. In descending order the results of this experiment were:

> happiness
> surprise
> fear
> love
> suffering
> disgust
> bewilderment
> anger
> determination
> contempt

Women, at least in this experiment, scored higher than men in using their faces to communicate happiness, love, fear, and anger. Men were more effective in expressing determination.

Teachers of special children, such as the emotionally disturbed, should not expect their students to make different kinds of faces from normal children. Rather, they may notice that special children make the same faces but for durations, at intensities, or in situations that are inappropriate.

Advertisers have learned to use the human face as a persuader. Some of their discoveries might have utility in the classroom. The faces of aloof-looking beautiful women in magazine advertisements, for example, attract more reader attention but sell fewer products. Photographs of brunettes receive more attention from women than photographs of blondes. According to reader surveys, brunettes have more "class," they talk slower, and are taller than blondes—at least in the minds of the public. Consequently brunettes are usually found selling the more sophisticated, serious products and blondes advertising the "fun" items. Reader surveys also indicate that "prettiness" in men is considered uninteresting. And strangely enough, in advertising, pictures of women draw the most attention from women, and men from men.

The human face is a viable, versatile instrument for sending information to other humans. The ordinary citizen is free to speculate about and interpret human facial expressions in any way that suits his fancy. A teacher does not and should not have that degree of freedom because subconscious biases often affect conscious behavior. Dr. Elaine Walster, a sociologist at the University of Wisconsin, has studied the attitudes of elementary school teachers toward attractive and unattractive children. She found that teachers believe that handsome and beautiful children are more intelligent, more sociable, more talented, and will usually do better than unattractive children. Needless to say, there is not a shred of evidence to support their belief. Talent and intelligence, like the rain, fall indiscriminately on the good, the bad, the beautiful, and the ugly.

The danger here, of course, is that teachers' expectations strongly influence student behavior. Thus the unattractive child is placed in double jeopardy. Not only must he fight an unsympathetic culture for his place in the sun, he must also overcome the subconscious bias of one whom he thinks is a friend, his teacher. This is a terrible burden for small children to carry, but luckily, it is one that sympathetic teachers can lift from students today.

FOR FURTHER READING

Andrew, R. J. "The Evolution of Facial Expressions." *Science*, Nov. 22, 1963, vol. 142, no. 3595, pp. 1034–51.

———. "The Origins of Facial Expressions." *Scientific American*, Oct. 1965, vol. 213, no. 4, pp. 88–94.

Bakan, Paul. "The Eyes Have It." *Psychology Today*, April 1971, vol. 4, no. 11, pp. 64–7.

Birdwhistell, Ray L. *Kinesics and Context*. Philadelphia: University of Pennsylvania Press, 1970.

Darwin, Charles. *The Expression of the Emotions in Man and Animals*. New York: Philosophical Library, 1955.

Ekman, Paul and Friesen, Wallace V. "Nonverbal Leakage and Clues to Deception." *Psychiatry*, vol. 32, no. 1, 1969, pp. 88–106.

———, ———, and Ellsworth, P. *The Face and Emotions: Guidelines for Research and Integration of Findings*. New York: Pergamon Press, 1971.

Ford, Barbara. "Who's Beautiful to Whom—and Why." *Science Digest*, Jan. 1971, pp. 9–14.

Froman, Robert. *The Great Reaching Out: How Living Beings Communicate*. Cleveland: World, 1968.

Hess, Eckhard H. "Attitude and Pupil Size." *Scientific American*, April 1965, vol. 212, no. 4, pp. 46–54.

Sakurano, Tomoko. "Mysteries of the Orient: What Your Lips Tell About You." *World of Fashions*, Tokyo: Bunka Fukuso Gakvin, summer 1970, pp. 90–1.

POSTURAL
COMMUNICATION

After years of observing students of all ages at work and play, many teachers have concluded that the human body seems to be capable of almost infinite posturing. They might be tempted to speculate that human posture is idiosyncratic. Each student seems to pose, move, and position his body in his own way and for no apparent reason. But if human posture is idiosyncratic and if the human body is capable of posing in an infinite number of ways, then analysis would be practically impossible. So at the outset of this inquiry into the language of human posture, an important assumption must be made—posture, like facial expression, is logical, patterned, and predictable. It *can* be analyzed.

Analysis is possible because human posture is, in fact, neither infinite nor completely idiosyncratic. The skeletal and muscle structure of the body will permit it to assume only about one thousand different steady postures. A steady posture is one that may be held comfortably for some time. One thousand different postures may seem to be a large number, but it is far from infinite and certainly manageable in terms of gathering and analyzing data.

Human posture is not idiosyncratic for a number of reasons. First, although a person's body may be capable of assuming many different postures, his culture, his profession, and even his circle of social acquaintances may not permit him to assume some postures. For example, Americans are not permitted by culture to stand on one leg like the legendary Nile River tribesmen. Undoubtedly Americans could learn to do it, but in their culture they may not. In some small rural communities in Georgia, men are permitted to squat on their heels in the company of other men on the sidewalk in front of the local general store. But if they lived in New York City, squatting in front of stores would not be acceptable behavior. And, of course, if one is a teacher, colleagues and friends expect one to stand, sit, and walk in certain ways. Construction workers are supposed to pose their bodies in virile ways, fashion models must be graceful and poised, and politicians must be friendly and outgoing. In short, people are not free to do as they please. There is strong pressure to conform to social expectations.

Another important damper on human posture is sex. A person's sex frequently dictates the ways he may pose his body. For example, a man may not stand like a woman, and a woman may not sit like a man. Male-like clothing on women and the longer hair styles of men in recent years have brought about some blurring of these once distinct male-female postures. It is now not uncommon to find a woman, legs elevated, relaxing on a park bench or a man tossing the hair out of his eyes. Nevertheless, the general male-female postures still prevail, and people may ignore them at their social peril.

There may also be genetic dampers, as yet undiscovered, that further restrict posture. It is not inconceivable, for example, that the Nile River tribesman, through natural selection, has been "programmed" to sustain a one-legged stance much better than Americans, or that Americans may better be suited to maintain an upright sitting posture for longer periods of time than the Chinese. At the present time there are few clear cut lines separating learned behavior from "wired-in" behavior. Hopefully, further study will clarify these perplexing issues.

There is little doubt, however, that most human posturing or "body language" is a logical, predictable set of behaviors through which humans communicate their deep feelings to anyone who can understand the language. Like facial expression, body language occurs generally at the subconscious level with neither sender nor receiver consciously aware of the messages passing between them. Yet being able to send and receive these messages is so important that until one learns to do it, one is not culturally mature. For example, a person may master the French language and speak and write it fluently, yet a six-year-old French child may easily mark him as a foreigner. He may not have learned French "body language." Similarly, children of American subcultures such as blacks, Indians, and Mexican-Americans are sometimes at a disadvantage in a school setting because they may have learned a different "dialect" of American body language and may either misunderstand or be misunderstood when bodies converse. Flare-ups of racial conflict in newly integrated schools, for example, are frequently caused by misunderstandings of body language. Customary postures of black students may be interpreted as threatening by white students, or the casual posturing of whites may frequently be interpreted by blacks as negative and offensive. These misunderstandings will disappear as students learn to understand each other's language systems.

Body language is a swift, sure way of communicating between members of the same culture or species. In some animal species learning to use it accurately and fluently is literally a matter of life and death. The flight maneuvers of starlings is an excellent example.

The mortal enemy of starlings is the falcon. The falcon ranges high above the starling flock, waiting for a straggler. Then with devastating swiftness he dives, embedding his talons in his prey. But starlings have learned some defensive maneuvers that are equally effective. When a falcon is in the vicinity, the starling flock draws together, wingtip to wingtip. So tightly packed is the flock that the falcon dares not dive. He has learned that to collide with such a densely packed flock at speeds of 150 miles an hour may shatter the fragile bones of his wings. And so he hovers and waits as the starlings perform their complicated, evasive maneuvers. How does each individual starling know when the flock is going to turn, dive, swirl, or climb? The starling has become an excellent sender and receiver of body communication. If an individual should zig while the flock zags, the falcon has him. Natural selection insures that only the best body communicators will survive.

The human situation, though not as urgent, is just as important. Body language adds a unique dimension to human communication that must be considered to understand the total message. If for any reason body language is not learned or is learned inaccurately or incompletely, the consequences may be difficult to overcome. In a sense, "disadvantaged" is a rather fancy word for an impoverishment of communication between a person from a poor socio-economic background and the larger community in which he lives. Any time an individual moves from one culture or subculture to another, he is bound to be disadvantaged until he masters the language system. Imagine the confusion of a robin who happens to blunder into the middle of a maneuvering starling flock? Or the confusion of the starlings? Part of a teacher's job is to ameliorate these differences among his students so that robins may fly with starlings.

Although body language must be considered in context with verbal language to derive meaning, there are times when bodies converse intensely without words, and other times when body language may contradict words. A good actor may lend credence to his words by supporting it with appropriate body language. He is a professional liar. A poor actor, on the other hand, may not have learned to add the body language dimension, or, even worse, his body language may contradict his words. Prominent sports figures who perform in television commercials are frequently guilty of this kind of amateur fibbing.

As the language of body posture is explored, gaps and inconsistencies in the data will be noticed. This, of course, is frustrating to all students of body language. If teachers will remember, however, that only a decade or so ago body language was practically unheard of, perhaps they will not judge too harshly a new field of human study that holds so much promise for a better understanding of human behavior.

Posturing in Groups

One of the most common types of body language is *disengagement*. If a person is watching television intently, for example, he has probably assumed a posture compatible with the kinds of feelings the television show is arousing in him. If the action is fast and tense, he may be leaning forward, body tense, eyes fixed on the TV screen. Suppose the action reaches a climax and then slows down. Chances are, he will shift his posture to reflect the slower tempo of the program. He disengages. He may turn his head or his body away from the television set and allow his attention momentarily to be directed elsewhere. These temporary shifts of posture away from the center of events and toward a new center of interest are examples of disengagement.

Every role a person assumes—speaker, listener, critic, sympathizer—is usually accompanied by a certain posture. These are his multiple identities, and they may change thousands of times during his waking day. As his role changes, the position of his body changes. He disengages from one set of events to engage in another. Each event is accompanied by its postural markers. For example, the really great trial lawyers, through subtly executed postural shifts, may "wring out" a jury emotionally during the course of a final summation. They may be accusing, sympathetic, wrathful, forgiving, angry, logical, solicitous, vengeful—depending on the mood they are trying to arouse in the jurors. And their posture eloquently and easily shifts from one emotional identity to another.

Teachers may notice that students in their classes frequently disengage during class period. As class discussion changes tempo or shifts direction, students may change posture accordingly. Frequently, too, teachers may notice that individual students disengage at various times. Disengagement may take the form of a shift in posture or direction of the body away from the teacher and perhaps toward a door or window. This is a body message signifying that the student has had enough of the teacher for a while. Teachers should realize that this is a normal and natural thing to do. In fact, teachers themselves may just as frequently disengage from their students. The wide open space beyond the windows is a tempting lure for students' attention, and teachers should expect students to gaze occasionally at the freedom beyond the classroom walls. Even penned turkeys frequently face toward the wire of their enclosure. If the disengagement is only temporary, no harm is done. However, if disengagement is frequent and prolonged, it is time for the teacher to ask himself some serious questions about his own performance.

People use their bodies to invite certain people to join them and to exclude others. These particular body postures have been labeled *exclusive* and *non-exclusive*. A person may attend a cocktail party or a church social and arrive when things are already underway. He will probably find small groups of people congregating at various points throughout the room, and each standing group forms a circle. In fact, all standing groups tend to form circles, and the purpose of the circle is to exclude unwelcome outsiders. The members of each group position their bodies in such a way that the group is closed to outside intervention.

When a person enters a room and finds people so engaged, he will probably seek out someone who, like himself, has been excluded. They will begin their own circle. Or perhaps he will be lucky, and one of the circles will open up to receive him. Relieved, he will now become part of the circle and use his own body to help shore-up the defense perimeter.

Occasionally a group is forced to stand in line, for example on a refreshment or reception line. It would seem as though a group would have to give up its circle and become open to everyone. Not so. These exclusive groups are easy to identify. The members at each end will usually turn inward so that they face each other and enclose the other group members. Further, the members at each end may extend an arm or leg across the open space to limit access to the group. Generally, the end positions will be assumed by males of the highest status. If a person is forced to break through the line to go to the door, he will not usually break through the middle of one of these groups. Subconsciously he will search the line for the postural markers that signify the end of a group. At that point he may break the line without arousing too much indignation.

Students in classes may group themselves in many ways—by interest, by ability, by sex, perhaps even by race. Teachers should be able to identify the closed groups. As noted in the earlier chapter on work space, a teacher may have to be arbitrary in composing work groups for maximum effectiveness and efficiency. It is doubtful, however, if he can impose a lasting structure on social groups. A good teacher will attempt to create the kind of in-class climate that is open, threat-free, and tolerant of differences. Over a period of time, if the climate is right, students may be willing to open up their tight social groups. Above all, teachers must see to it that individual students, especially students of minority races and cultures, belong to some group. There is nothing quite so distressing to human beings of all ages as to be excluded from social interaction, to be constantly on the outside. It erodes a student's self-confidence and pride and will surely affect both his work and the teacher's. If a teacher watches carefully for the postural markers, he should be able to identify the groups that are usually closed and the individuals who are usually excluded. Identifying them could be the first important step toward remediation.

Teachers may notice that groups of students in their class tend to hold their heads and extremities in the same position. It is not uncommon, for example, to find an entire row of students with their legs crossed. If a teacher asked one of the students why he crossed his legs, he would probably answer that he "just felt like it." Yet an entire row would not "feel like" crossing their legs at exactly the same time. Similarly, a teacher might find a group of students with their arms folded or another group resting their chins on their hands. It is beyond coincidence that so many people should decide to do exactly the same thing at exactly the same time. This is a behavioral phenomenon peculiar to all groups known as *congruent posture.*

Members of a group often hold their heads and extremities—feet, legs, hands and arms—in the same position. Congruent posture indicates that the group (or subgroup) holds a common point of view or that there is a similarity of roles among members. An entire row of students may cross their legs at the same time because they share some common feelings about what is going on in the class and their relationship at the moment to each other and to the instructor. Usually a leader will initiate the posture for the group, and the other members will follow. If a teacher is patient and observant, he may be able to identify the leaders. They are the ones who shift posture first.

Frequently a subgroup within a larger group will develop a point of view of its own. This subgroup may then assume a congruent posture of its own. Thus in a typical class a teacher may find a large group with legs crossed, a smaller subgroup with arms folded, and another subgroup with hands clasped, plus a few mavericks who may not agree with anyone. When a different point of view develops within a group, usually the members holding that point of view will assume incongruent posture with the larger group.

Sometimes in family psychotherapy a counselor finds the same kind of division within a family. As the family sits in the counselor's office, one child may assume congruent posture with one parent, while the other children may do so with the other parent. If the counselor is familiar with body language, he may immediately suspect that the family is divided over some ideational or affective issues. The division begins with the parents, and the children have chosen sides. The counselor may also read body language to determine when the family is once again a functioning, cohesive unit. All the members may assume congruent posture with each other.

People in authority may use incongruent posture to

remind subordinates of their lower status. If a teacher observes his own behavior carefully, he may find that subconsciously he assumes an incongruent posture with groups of students or individuals. This is his way of "putting students in their place." Physicians sometimes assume incongruent posture with patients for the same reason, and supervisors with teachers.

Simply by noting the congruency of posture when students work in groups, teachers may be able to determine which groups are functioning well and which may require attention. They might try calling on the "incongruent" students for their contribution.

In small groups of three people there is a tendency for two to sit parallel, both facing the third individual. In groups of four, each set of two will usually sit facing the other twosome. Face-to-face positions are used to exchange personal information and feelings. If a person is sincerely interested in what another person has to say, he will probably face him. If, on the other hand, information is being exchanged about a third party or an event taking place some distance away, people will usually stand or sit in body-parallel positions.

People do strange things to juggle two interesting but opposite events at the same time. Suppose, for example, a girl is conversing with two boys whom she likes equally well. Further, imagine that all three are seated on a couch with the girl in the middle. If she turns to face one boy, she may alienate the other. How does she solve this dilemma? She divides her body in two. The upper half may face in the direction of one boy while the lower half faces toward the other. In this way she manages to satisfy both and keep the group together.

The systematic analysis of human posture has come

into prominence largely through the work of Dr. Albert E. Scheflen, a psychiatrist, and Ray Birdwhistell, an anthropologist. Scheflen's basic premise is that body posture is a communicative act rather than a personality variable. In other words, people pose their bodies in certain ways to send subconscious messages and not because they happen to possess particular personality characteristics. If the premise is valid, then one would expect to find patterns of posture that are common to most people in a culture who are sending similar messages. The studies of both men demonstrate that such is the case. Most human posturing is patterned and predictable.

Individual Posture

Tenseness and relaxation, especially in their extremes, are accurate postural markers. Whenever men or women face people or situations that evoke deep personal feelings, their bodies respond in predictable fashion. Men grow tense when confronted by other threatening men. If the other men pose little threat but are disliked, then a man may over-relax in their presence. Women, on the other hand, show dislike for other women and men through extreme relaxation. Humans display interest in each other through moderate tenseness. When a person first meets someone who is attractive, he will usually become tense. When he grows accustomed to someone, however, when the excitement is gone and everything has become "old hat," he may demonstrate his lack of interest by over-relaxing in the other's presence. This is a constant complaint of many wives about their husbands, by the way.

The thought may occur that relaxation is a relative matter. What to someone may appear to be moderate relaxation, may to someone else seem to be extreme. Psychologist Albert Mehrabian has defined relaxation in a useful, operational way. When seated, extreme relaxation means that an individual has assumed a reclining angle greater than 20 degrees and a sideways lean greater than 10 degrees. Moderate relaxation, which in a sense means also moderate tenseness, requires a forward lean greater than 20 degrees and a sideways lean of less than 10 degrees. Extreme tenseness may be identified by a rigid, upright posture with perhaps a slight forward lean and an extreme tenseness of the muscles of the hands.

Students who are called on to address the class may exhibit all the classic symptoms of tension, especially high school students in the upper grades. Naturally, a teacher expects all students to respond when they are addressed directly. It is doubtful, however, if a tense student can offer his best efforts. If tense students can be identified, a teacher might try to put them at ease by a relaxed atmosphere and a high tolerance for mistakes and misjudgments. Some teachers conduct an inquisition rather than an open, friendly question-and-answer session. Students who are prone to tenseness and anxiety are the first casualties in these harrowing encounters.

Occasionally a teacher may come across a student who shows his disdain for both teacher and class through extreme relaxation. He is probably the more difficult case to deal with. If a student dislikes a teacher, dislikes the class, and perhaps dislikes the whole school situation, there isn't much a teacher alone can do about it. Unfortunately such a girl or boy may sometimes be among the brighter students. This slouching, bored student is a casualty of mass education and outmoded curriculums. It is futile to nag him about his sloppy posture and lack of interest. Posture is not a personality trait—it is a body message, in this case signifying boredom. If a teacher can engage him in some worthwhile activity and arouse his interest, his posture may correct itself.

Individuals in a large group sometimes seek out other individuals to carry on business not directly related to the work of the group. A couple may splinter off to engage in argumentation or discussion or to carry on a private flirtation. If the group is highly task-oriented, these private bits of business by individual members are resented by other members who may take preventive action. If the group is seated, a leg may be thrust between the offending couple by a third member. If standing, a third member may maneuver part of his body—an arm or shoulder, for example—between them. In each instance the larger group, through one or more of its members, is attempting to limit individual behavior so that the group may work toward task completion with as much cohesion as possible.

An argumentative or belligerent individual within a group may be controlled in a similar way. Frequently members on each side will box him in with their legs. In an established group new male members may find access to females blocked with bodies, parts of bodies, or even chairs. The group frowns on private male-female business until the newcomer has established himself and demonstrated his good intentions. Since not all male-female couples are flirtatious, however, there needs to be a set of markers that such couples may use to demonstrate to the larger group that their liaison is purely for business or social purposes. If men and women are seated closely in non-intimate, social situations, they will tend to cross their legs or lean back from each other, or both. This is their way of stating, "See, everything is on the up and up here."

Between the couple themselves there is a set of cues by which one may tell the other to keep the conversation friendly and nonintimate. The voice level is usually raised, signifying that anyone who wants to may listen. If one person gazes too long at the other, the gaze is not returned. During conversation frequent references to wife, husband, or children serve notice to the other person that no flirtation is intended or desired.

If the opposite is the case, however, and a couple wishes to be left alone, they will usually face together, lean toward each other, and try to block entry by a third party by using their arms or crossing their feet to close the circle. Subconsciously these signals are usually correctly interpreted by the third party, who may decide to leave them alone or break up the flirtation for the good of the group. If a third party decides to move in on the couple, they may show their resentment toward the intruder by assuming congruent posture. They may cross their legs or fold their arms. Sometimes they may keep the lower half of their bodies turned toward each other while the upper half faces the third person. They are saying emphatically through body language, "You cannot separate us. We are still together in spite of you."

If a teacher should find himself the third party in classroom flirtations and if he has decided that for the good of the group such flirtations must cease, he will have to be firm but diplomatic in his insistence that classroom business take precedence over private affairs.

He may do this by quietly asking the students to return to work. He may have to repeat his request two or three times before the couple complies. It may also be possible to use group pressure to keep students from splintering off into private parties. If a class is task-oriented and there is a sense of urgency and commitment, the group can bring persuasive pressure to bear on members who refuse to carry their fair share of the work.

A teacher's own body posture frequently signals to his students much of his feelings about them and his work. Because he has read about and perhaps is able to identify some postural markers in others, a teacher should not assume that he is himself immune to communication through body language. If he consciously sets out to control some aspects of his body language, he may succeed for a time. But in the long run, unless he is an extremely talented actor, sooner or later his body will signal to others how he really feels about them. For example, if when a teacher addresses a class, he feels very positive about what he is saying, he will lean toward the class. Knowing this, suppose he decides to always give the impression that he believes what he is saying by leaning forward. But if this teacher tries to lean toward the group when he has negative feelings, he will discover that a conscious, determined effort is required. Rest assured that if he "fakes" it, sooner or later his body will give the lie to his words and his credibility will be diminished. A person simply cannot consciously control total body behavior for long. The only answer is to mean what one says. Sometimes students may not like it, but they will know exactly where the teacher and they stand—an important characteristic of effective human relations.

Both men and women frequently use their body orientation to tell another person that they have more status. Both men and women will probably avoid direct body orientation toward women of lower status. This means that when an individual engages a woman of inferior status in conversation, he will approach her from an angle and will maintain this angle until the conversation ends. Strangely enough, men of lower status are treated in a completely opposite manner. One's body will directly confront their body. These maneuverings, of course, are performed and observed subconsciously. Nevertheless, the message is understood by the other person, although he or she may not be able to verbalize exactly how it was received. Now if a teacher's words preach equality and brotherhood while his body preaches inequality and servitude, no one need remind him which message carries the most weight. Again, the only answer is to mean what one says or keep silent. A person's body speaks eloquently for itself.

There are some characteristic elements of male posture with which teachers, especially female teachers, should be familiar. Males and females experience the world in different ways. They structure space differently and use their bodies differently to express their feelings. Unless a female teacher has had some experience with the behavioral characteristics of adolescent and postadolescent males, misunderstandings between the teacher and her male students are bound to occur.

The "male-defiant" stance of adolescent males is an excellent example of the kind of posture that frequently upsets the unknowing female teacher. If a female teacher has reason to speak sternly to a high school male, he may stand spread-legged, thumbs in belt, just daring the teacher, nonverbally, to do her worst. The wise teacher will go out of her way to unruffle this anxious young man. He has assumed his pre-fight posture and is ready to do battle. This pose is characteristic of adolescent males—and of some males years beyond the age of adolescence. He is not defying the teacher, personally. He is simply exerting his male prerogative of standing up to authority. This same stance, by the way, also marks his pre-sexual advances. Adolescent male students may sometimes confront young female teachers with this posture. Actually, they have little conscious awareness of the significance of their behavior. They are "trying out" the heady stuff of maleness. A teacher's understanding, patience, maturity, and a high sense of professionalism will help these young men put the world and their role in it in proper perspective.

In American culture, males have a low tolerance for body contact with each other. Arab or French males may embrace or even kiss on certain occasions, but native-born American males demand lots of space and little body contact. If a female teacher wishes to make her male high school students thoroughly uncomfortable in a small group situation, she may simply seat them so that they are crowded and cannot avoid body contact. In that case they may turn away from each other and cross their legs. That is their signal to her to do something to relieve the pressure of bodies.

Female teachers are frequently unaware of the lower tolerance of male students for body contact. Equality of the sexes does not mean that a teacher must assign an equal amount of space to a 110 pound female and a 190 pound male. If that happens, carefully aligned rows of chairs will soon disappear in an apparently unequal distribution of space as the class seeks its own spatial equilibrium. Custodians have a low tolerance for that sort of disorder and will usually arrange the chairs in equal rows again, unless the teacher intervenes on behalf of her students.

The "selling" posture of males is another common behavioral characteristic that teachers may sometimes observe. Sitting back in a chair rarely occurs in subordinate males who are pressing a point or selling an idea to a male of high status. When male students join in small group discussion, a teacher may be able to identify the leader of the group simply by observing the posture of other males as they address him.

Certainly there is ample evidence on hand to explode forever the myth of male supremacy. Actually, males are vulnerable, sensitive human beings who have been forced by culture and tradition to display physical and emotional strengths they frequently do not possess. That women have now uncovered this ancient fiction is regarded by many males with resignation and no small relief. The masquerade is over at last. Today's male is different. He, too, has been liberated. He expects to be treated equally—but differently, even in schools.

If the world is male-dominated, as some females claim with just indignation, then the public schools, especially the elementary schools, are female-dominated. Both need changing. There are too many males, abdominal muscles sagging in depression, stalking the corridors of medical clinics, victims of their own mythology. Just as females need champions to advance their cause in a male-oriented society, so male students need champions in a female-oriented public school system. Today's teacher, aware that males and females are different, must seek ways to insure that both sexes advance, and not one at the expense of the other. Male students do need a champion.

Sometimes the emotional condition of students may harden their bodies in rigid patterns. A belligerent, aggressive student, male or female, may walk or sit with head thrust forward. An unhappy student may frown continuously. Sometimes the class situation itself may evoke general postural shifts from everyone. For example, if a teacher is ever in doubt as to when to stop lecturing to a class, their gross body movements and postural shifts will inform him that his time is up. As a class period draws to a close, the teacher may be tempted to cram as much material as possible into the few remaining minutes. Students resent this. They will frown and fuss, stretch, squirm, and slam their notebooks. Their message is clear: "End it now!" Little is gained by driving furiously down to the closing seconds, and even less by going overtime. A teacher who habitually exceeds the time limit of the class earns the resentment of students and colleagues. Students need the few intervening minutes between classes to relax, disengage, and prepare for the next assignment. Only an insensitive teacher will deprive them of their well-earned respite.

Furniture and Postural Behavior

Humans as social groups have survived because they have been able to devise effective communication systems, but the purpose of these systems has not always been to transmit truth. Rather, the basic purpose is group and personal survival. Not infrequently, truth becomes a casualty if a social group's basic survival is threatened. Some individuals may express alarm and indignation at the games people play with truth, but sometimes survival is more important than any particular truth.

For instance, a bored student soon learns that to look bored and uninterested invites academic disaster. Thus, he camouflages his boredom with what he thinks are appropriate looks and postures of interest. He survives at the expense of truth. There may come a time in man's evolution when such deception is no longer necessary, but that time has not yet arrived. Whether in international diplomacy, social relations, or in classroom contacts, people usually place their own personal and group survival above particular and perhaps unimportant truths. Certainly there is ample precedent in nature for doing so.

There are orchids that trick flies into carrying their pollen; fish that lure and trap other fish; birds that camouflage themselves and their nests; and snakes that play "dead." It should come as no surprise, then, that nature's most precocious child, man, has become an expert at manipulating truth to achieve and maintain his own personal equilibrium. In the late 1940's when commercial television was in its infancy, owning a television set was a status symbol of some importance. It was not uncommon to find roof top antennas whose lead-in wires led nowhere. The important thing was to erect the antenna and keep up with the neighbors. The TV would come later when finances permitted.

At this time in man's evolution, to be truthful consistently, regardless of the consequences, could be disasterous. It is doubtful if our social, economic, and political institutions could stand the strain. Words such as "diplomacy," "tact," "white lies," "national security," and others attest to the need for something less than truth when certain conditions prevail. A significant part of growing up in a culture is learning how much truth to tell to whom, and when. Indeed how much truth to tell one's self is sometimes a moot question.

In searching for the meaning of human nonverbal behavior, then, things are not always what they seem. People camouflage themselves and their acts in ingenious ways with layer upon layer of little deceits designed to throw the casual observer off the track. The purpose is to survive, to keep one's self intact.

Sometimes people use the furniture in homes and public places to help them manage truth. For example, among upper-income families, there are those who feel comfortable with their status and those who do not. But the very ones who feel uneasy are frequently the ones who play it "coolest." To find truth one must look beyond the behavioral fascade. In this case, the family living room may provide some important clues.

There is some evidence that families who are well established in their life style, who hold well-defined views on politics, religion, leisure, and other important issues, and who have clear cut notions of man-woman roles, tend toward traditional decor in their living rooms. On the other hand, families new to their income and status, who are climbing socially, and who conspicuously consume goods tend toward a living room decorated in the modern style. In neither case is the living room given over to television viewing. This is now associated with families of lower income.

Occasionally truth is managed in public places by

manipulating furniture and fixtures. Attractive signs and pleasant aromas of the standing breakfast and lunch bars of quickie eating establishments in large cities invite patrons in, but high density packing and lack of chairs discourage them from lingering. And it is actually possible to manipulate customer turnover in bars and restaurants by increasing or decreasing illumination. As illumination increases, noise levels rise and patrons depart. On a slow night the proprietor may wish to keep his few customers lingering at their tables. Lowered illumination may do the trick. Perhaps the ultimate in the manipulation of customers by furniture is a chair for coffee shops designed in Sweden and now being marketed in the United States. The chair looks comfortable and inviting. After a few minutes, however, it exerts disagreeable pressure upon the spine of the customer who quickly finishes his coffee and departs, unaware that the furniture has prompted his hasty exit.

A teacher may notice that students often use school furniture to send messages. The student who wishes to be left alone, for example, tends to seat himself away from the door. This is especially true in cafeteria or social room situations. Surprisingly, most people subconsciously recognize this nonverbal message and respect it. Even a teacher will hesitate before breaking into this student's private world.

In classroom work involving the use of tables, teachers may occasionally observe a student who does not wish to share his table. He lays claim to it by planting himself solidly at the center, facing the door. Teachers may observe the same student in the cafeteria putting on a similar performance. In both cases the student is strongly asserting his right to his own table.

Benches offer another opportunity for people to pose their bodies in ways that reflect their feelings. If there are benches on the school campus, teachers may observe a student who takes over an entire bench by seating himself directly in the center. Most students will usually prefer to stand or sit on the ground rather than directly challenge the occupant for a share of the bench. Then there is the student who seats himself at one end of the bench. His bench position says, "You may share this bench if you wish, but keep as far away as possible and don't bother me."

Finally, and most frequently, teachers may notice that most students wish to share their bench with others. They indicate this by sitting off-center, leaving the center space open for anyone who wishes to socialize with them.

Because of the peculiar bench behavior of people, long benches may be inefficient. Two people, one at each end, may effectively close the bench to further occupancy. Professional decorators need to rethink the design of furniture in terms of people's peculiar quirks of behavior. "Two's company; three's a crowd" is what the evidence indicates.

Thus as people interact with the furniture and fixtures in the environment, their body positions convey information. Sometimes this information is meant to transmit their real feelings to others, perhaps at a subconscious level. But sometimes intentional misinformation is passed along to confuse or deceive the observer. A teacher's task is to sort out this confusing welter of information, realizing all the while that deceptive behavior is survival behavior, and that behind each deception, there is a reason and a logic. If teachers are ever to understand why students behave as they do, they must try to discover the totality, the complete context, of the situation. Whether quietly cheating on an exam or aggressively pushing to the front of the lunch room line, students, it must be assumed, are acting logically and rationally, although perhaps subconsciously. Teachers must look for the logic and the reason. They may not agree with the logic or condone the reason, but that is irrelevant. As students of behavior, they must first try to determine the nature of the situation as objectively as possible. Then as teachers they may wish to do something about it. But it is well to remember which comes first.

Clothing and Behavior

One may buy clothing at many prices and select from many styles. Some female students may dress for comfort; others may be extremely fashion-conscious. Some may prefer to go along with the majority, and still others may look for bargains rather than the latest fashions.

Do these choices, if made consistently, represent unique personality types? Perhaps. A study of University of North Carolina coeds revealed that girls who choose their garments for comfort and practicality tend to be self-controlled, dependable, and socially well adjusted. They are certainly not boat-rockers nor are they the ones who stand up to or defy authority.

On the other hand, girls who are style and fashion-conscious, who cannot bear the thought of attending this year's dance in last year's dress, are for the most part conscientious but conventional. They think in stereotypes and may best be described, perhaps, as non-intellectuals. They are sympathetic toward people and their problems. These are the girls one usually finds socializing in the coffee shop during free periods. They are highly gregarious.

Another type of girl may choose her clothing to conform to that of the majority, regardless of what the style setters and fashion-conscious wear. She prefers not to stand out. Generally, she is conservative in outlook and traditional in her approach to life. She regards money and good social standing as objects of great value. She probably has little concern for the arts and literature.

Finally, another group of girls choose their clothing in terms of thrift and economy. These girls wait for clearance sales and out-of-season mark-downs. As a group, they tend to be conscientious, alert, efficient, precise, and in full control of their destinies. They are intelligent, the kind of students most teachers enjoy working with—the curious, the truth-seekers, the persistent scholars.

The effects of clothing on posture and behavior (or vice versa) is a new avenue for serious investigation. If current data are reliable, the selection of clothing provides some insights into a person's way of looking at the world. Sometimes clothing is an extension of a person's personality patterns and conscious or subconscious desires. One's costume for a fancy dress ball, for example, may indeed reflect one's own subconscious wishes in some symbolic form. Sometimes, on the other hand, clothing itself may shape behavior. Is it a mere coincidence that sloppily dressed children tend to get into mischief and commit nuisances? The same children, when dressed up, usually change their behavior to conform to their attire.

If school administrators based their clothing regula-
tions on research data rather than on such abstract notions as "good taste," they would be on firmer ground.
Does sloppy and unusual dress beget sloppy, disruptive
behavior? The evidence seems to point that way. If a
change in behavior can bring about a change in clothing, is it unreasonable to suppose that a change in
clothing may bring about a change in behavior?

In Chapter 7 the significance of the skin in human
communication will be discussed. Clothing is next to
the skin, in intimate contact with it. People extend beyond their skin and into their clothing. Some mornings
a teacher may feel alert and eager to get on with the
day's work. On other mornings he may feel depressed
or discouraged. In either case, he will probably select
his wardrobe for the day to match his mood. It is not an
accident that psychiatric counselors consider an interest
in grooming one of the most favorable signs. When a
patient finally looks for a comb or a change of clothing,
the counselor regards this as one of the favorable signs
of recovery.

Even the particular dress associated with certain oc-
cupations is meant to convey definite information about
the occupation and its practitioners. The engineering
student with a slide rule hanging from his belt or the
medical student with his stethoscope protruding from
the pocket of his lab coat are telling people that their's
are exacting professions requiring precise instruments
and unusual abilities. Lab coats are themselves a form
of dress that frequently affects the behavior of the
wearer. In London chimney sweeps and perfume clerks
wear white lab coats. In the United States the lab coat
is the standard uniform of the health professions. As

soon as one dons a lab coat, however, there is a tendency to behave as though delicate tasks will be performed in a standardized, clinical, and confidential manner.

Do "clothes make the man"? Perhaps. There is some evidence that people who cannot find clothes to suit them usually cannot find jobs, friends, or anything else to suit them. A person is what he wears, and what he wears, in turn, tends to reinforce his own and other's expectations of what he ought to be.

FOR FURTHER READING

Ardrey, Robert. *The Social Contract*, New York: Atheneum, 1970.

Birdwhistell, Ray. *Kinesics and Context*, Philadelphia: University of Pennsylvania, 1970.

Gibson, John E. "What Your Clothes Reveal About Your Personality." *Catholic Digest*, March 1970, pp. 55–7.

Goffman, Erving. *The Presentation of Self in Everyday Life*. New York: Doubleday, 1959.

Hewes, Gordon W. "The Anthropology of Posture." *Scientific American*, vol. 196, no. 2, Feb., 1967.

Hicks, Clifford B. "Hidden Habits of Women." *Today's Health*, vol. 45, no. 12, Dec. 1967, pp. 28–31.

Mehrabian, Albert. "Communication Without Words." *Psychology Today*, vol. 2, no. 4, Sept. 1968.

Scheflen, Albert E. "The Significance of Posture in Communication Systems." *Psychiatry*, Nov. 1964, vol. 27, pp. 316–31.

Sommer, Robert. *Personal Space*. Englewood Cliffs, N.J.: Prentice-Hall, 1959.

THE LANGUAGE
OF GESTURES

After all that has been said about the "wholeness" of behavior, one might well question the wisdom of separating posture and gestures. Any single behavior is embedded in a matrix of many other behaviors, all of which must be considered in deriving meaning. If a student waves hello as he passes on the street, his body has probably assumed a concomitant posture and his face an appropriate expression. If one or more of these accompanying behaviors is missing or not what one expects them to be, then one would have reason to doubt the sincerity of his gesture. The gesture alone is not a completely reliable index of meaning.

Gestures are studied as a separate class of behavior solely as an academic exercise that has some limited value. For example, the teacher of history may isolate the Industrial Revolution from the whole stream of history to analyze some cause-effect relationships that are unique to the industrialization of nations. This procedure has value only if, in the final analysis, the Industrial Revolution is viewed within the total historical context of the time. Similarly, the study of gestures is valuable if, when the analysis is completed, gestures are viewed within the context of total behavior.

Perhaps the term "gesture" as it is used here should be defined. A gesture is an expressive movement of the head or limbs. Expressive means that the movement itself has communicative value to someone or something capable of inferring meaning.

Gesturing as a complete language system is not unfamiliar to most people. There is the hand language of deaf mutes and, of course, the expressive sign languages of American Indians, Pacific Islanders, and other peoples. Not surprisingly, then, some of the earliest attempts to deal with the entire phenomenon of nonverbal communication were concentrated in the realm of gestures, their origins, meanings, and cultural variations.

Americans use approximately thirty different gestures that might be considered traditional. These and their variations are the gestures that shall be considered here. Not all of them have been studied in detail, but some of them, such as the handshake, are under serious investigation at the present time. Some other gestures in current use fall outside of the traditional category—the peace sign, the clenched fist, and the expressive gestures of today's young blacks, for example. Perhaps some of these will endure to enrich our repertory of future traditional gestures.

Unless a person is a talented actor or actress or unusually aware of his own body's and limbs' movements, most of his gestures are spontaneous and occur below the level of conscious awareness. However, even though gestures may occur subconsciously, they are still an integral part of what sociologist Erving Goffman calls "impression management." That is, gestures make a unique contribution to the impression of yourself, your attitudes, and values you wish to communicate to others. Now this impression may represent the "real" you or it may not. That is not important. What is important is that other people receive the impression you intend them to receive. For example, suppose during class discussion a student makes a remark that is hilariously funny but is in poor taste. You look stern and gesture to be quiet. Outwardly you have managed an impression of disapproval; inwardly you may chuckle at his humor, even if it is not in the best taste.

So gestures, like posture and facial expressions, may represent real feelings, camouflage real feelings, or misrepresent them entirely. Nor are humans unique in nature when they undertake these deceptions, as has been pointed out in the previous chapter. A chameleon camouflages itself with the colors of its environment; a puffing adder sometimes misrepresents itself as a cobra; and a person may shake his head "no" when he really means "yes." Politicians are frequently accused of "managing" truth, news media of "managing" news, and pollsters of "managing" opinion. In truth, most human beings wish to present themselves to the world in the best possible light, and gestures often assist them in attaining this goal.

Gesturing, then, is another sublanguage that may be studied in its own right, but this study will have little validity if considered out of context with the totality of behavior. The study of gesturing will begin with its most eloquent instrument of expression—the human hands.

A Show of Hands

In Robert Merle's fascinating novel, *The Day of the Dolphin*, the plot centers around the efforts of researchers to teach tame dolphins the use of human verbal language. When they finally succeed and are able to communicate with these intelligent creatures, the human investigators ask the dolphins what they most admire about humans. The dolphins' reply goes right to the core of human evolution, perhaps right to the heart of humanness. The dolphins answer, "Human hands."

For what is man without his hands? Hands lay brick upon brick to build civilizations. Hands make music, perform surgery, adjust delicate instruments, and weave intricate tapestries. Human hands open doors, tuck children into bed, and reach ahead in dark, unfamiliar places. Human hands helped shape the world and the people in it. Even in advanced technological societies, many machines only do clumsily and indelicately what human hands do gracefully and easily. Visitors to foreign lands discover that when verbal language breaks down, gestural language usually takes over. Just by using his hands an American is able to obtain a glass of water in Israel or a bottle of champagne in Paris. It is said that without their hands, Italians would be speechless. But then so would the French, the Spanish, and many other nationalities. The hand of man is everywhere evident. Small wonder, then, that humans reach out with their hands to touch and hold the hands of other humans.

When a person offers his hand to another, he expects it to be grasped with equal firmness. If it is not, he feels let down. He has offered one of the most intimate of human gestures and expects a similar return. Unfortunately, handshaking often becomes a mere formality with neither party expecting nor receiving much in the way of intimacy. The formal handshake is reminiscent of medieval times when combatants sometimes made truce by grasping each other's weapon hand. If teachers are careful observers, they may find these uneasy truce gestures being offered as handshakes in classrooms, offices, and social gatherings.

Since the hand is so intimately a part of the total person, what is done with the hand often reflects how a person feels about himself and the world. Graphology, the study of human handwriting as an indicator of personality, has been a popular pastime for centuries. More recently psychologists and psychiatrists have provided useful information about some famous artists through an analysis of their paintings—their use of lines, color, composition, and symbology. On a more mundane level, there is evidence that even the way a person offers his hand to others in a traditional handshake may provide clues to his own personality. Listed below are a number of handshake types and a few personality traits associated with each type. They might provide a springboard for some interesting discussion or investigation.

Dead pan handshaker—He doesn't smile, doesn't let his hand respond to the pressure of the other person's hand. Secretly he probably feels superior.

Rough handshaker—He wants to appear tough and out-going. He may be trying to hide his own feelings of insecurity.

Limp handshaker—His hand feels as though it has no bones or muscles at all. He probably has a negative outlook on life. This is the handshake of chronic pessimists, doubters, and people who habitually wear dark glasses.

Bone-crushing handshaker—He is out to impress people. Deep down, however, he may suffer from feelings of inferiority and emotional insecurity.

Hesitant handshaker—He doesn't know whether to offer his hand or not. He may begin but unless the other person quickly acknowledges the gesture, he will probably withdraw. He is usually indecisive about everything else in life.

Close-to-body handshaker—His elbow is bent at right angles and held quite close to the body. He never sticks his neck out, either. He is cautious and conservative.

Compulsive handshaker—He shakes everybody's hand at every opportunity. He may shake one's hand half a dozen times in as many days. He needs to be noticed and accepted by everyone.

Nongrip handshaker—He refuses to give his entire hand. You will have to be satisfied with just his fingers. He is telling you not to take his handshake too seriously. He really does not wish to become involved. This is the handshake some teachers offer to students whom they wish to keep at a distance. If a teacher has ever been offered this handshake, he will appreciate how his students feel when he offers such a hand to them.

Jackhammer handshaker—He pumps the hand in a series of short, mechanical jerks. Watch out. He is determined, rigid, strong willed, and inflexible.

Captive audience handshaker—He won't let your hand go until he feels that he has made his point. He may even grasp your forearm with his free hand to make doubly sure you do not slip from his grasp. He may be a salesman or a promoter. He is also an opportunist. This is the kind of fellow who will manipulate and use people to attain his own ends.

The psychodynamics of handshaking is a relatively new area of study. Even if the above generalizations are accepted as little more than hypotheses to be tested, a broad avenue of fruitful investigation will have been opened. Teachers should take the initiative in offering to shake hands with students and colleagues. They should not concern themselves with which type of handshake is best. The idea is to put people at ease, to be friendly, and helpful. The handshake will take care of itself. A friendly handshake given in the spirit of good will may work wonders with shy, belligerent, and even indifferent students. And teachers might try to be aware of the handshakes they receive in return. They could provide some valuable insights into students' hopes, fears, and frustrations.

Americans and the people of many other cultures frequently approve of the behavior of others by clapping their hands. It is said that hand clapping began as an ancient Japanese custom to awaken the gods before the start of prayer. Hand clapping as a gesture of approval is so entrenched in American culture that all speakers—even bad ones—expect to be applauded. Studio audiences are coached when to clap, even when there is little to applaud. Buyers at fashion shows have been known to applaud for styles they would not put in their own stores, just to deceive their competitors. It was not uncommon in ancient Rome for musical performers to load the gallery with professional handclappers. As a matter of fact, this practice persisted until quite recently at the Metropolitan Opera House in New York City and the great opera houses of Europe. Some stars used hired handclappers called claques to loudly applaud their every aria and duet. Even today cheerleaders at football and basketball games exort spectators to cheer and clap every successful play of their favorite team. Thus, through the ages hand clapping has usually signified approval, but not necessarily so.

One of the most intriguing riddles encountered in the study of human hands is left- and right-handedness. If chance accounted for the proportion of left- and right-handedness, there ought to be as many left-handed people as right-handed. This, however, seems not the case. Left-handed people number a mere eighteen percent of the population. Why?

In the 1960s an interesting theory was proposed. This theory was based on an earlier study that provided substantial evidence that the human infant is positively conditioned to the mother's heartbeat prenatally. When a recording of a heartbeat was played in the nursery, the infants in the experimental group cried less and gained more weight than a control group that did not hear the heartbeat. Evidently the therapeutic value of the heart rhythm, gained prenatally, could be transferred to the post-natal environment.

Now, there are two ways an infant might hear a heartbeat. One way is to record and play it back in the nursery, as the experimenters in the study demonstrated. The other way requires the mother to carry her infant on her left side, over the heart. But this is an awkward position for left-handed mothers. Consequently, more right-handed mothers than left- carry their babies on the left side. The theory mentioned above proposes that since there is therapeutic value in listening to the mother's heartbeat, infants who receive this therapy are more favored for survival. Further, since most children of right-handed mothers receive the therapy, they are healthier and stronger, and hence better able to survive and propagate right-handedness than are the offspring of left-handed mothers.

If, as the statistics seem to indicate, left-handed people are moving toward extinction, then perhaps they should be treated as any other species in similar danger. Alexander the Great, Babe Ruth, Michelangelo, and Charlemagne were great not because they were left-handed. It is enough that they were great *and* left-handed. Certainly the genetic influences that bring about left-handedness must in some unknown ways enrich and diversify a right-handed world. This is reason enough for preserving and encouraging left-handedness until more is learned about it.

Whether left- or right-handed, however, the unique human activity, learning to write, is an arduous task for children because grammarians would have them believe that writing is merely a way of recording words. As soon as a person puts his hand around a pencil, however, the motion of his body flows out of his hand and records information the grammarian is not prepared to deal with. The word "run," for example, is more than a written symbol. It is a series of intricate body motions, a feeling, an idea, a complexity of behavior, and a conceptualization. To expect all youngsters to write the word "run" in letters of uniform length, height, and spacing, as though their hands were mechanical devices attached to their bodies through a series of linkages, is to deny reality. Handwriting, which is a body motion and like all body motions is highly personal and subjective, is taught as though it has an existence apart from the hand and brain of the writer. Even typewriting displays the peculiarities of the machine that produced it.

If teachers wish children to learn to write easily and naturally, they must approach writing as a body motion activity as well as an exercise in grammar. If this means getting rid of all those "beautiful" penmanship models so prominently displayed in most elementary classrooms, then so be it. Most of them look as though they were made by robots anyway. Human handwriting was never meant to be, indeed cannot be, consistently uniform and predictable. If uniformity is desired, then typing, not writing, should be introduced in the first grade.

A more human and natural approach to writing is not all that is needed. A more realistic approach to grammar itself should be considered. What is "run"? "Run" is a verb, a part of speech, you say. Only in a textbook of English grammar is that so. In real life "run" is body motion. What kind of grammar is it that merely labels and never comes to grips with the fundamental idea the label is supposed to describe? No wonder children have difficulty with grammar. The grammarian's "grammar" is unreal, too narrow, and too abstract. Humans need a new science that will encompass the total human language, a living grammar for living people.

When Hands Converse

There are students of nonverbal communication who believe that the hands alone offer the best cues to human deceptive behavior. They claim, on the basis of some evidence, that the face can be controlled to a large extent. If a person is fearful and does not wish to show fear, for example, he may control his facial expression. People commonly control facial expressions of anger, surprise, joy, sorrow, and other basic human emotions with much or little success depending on how practiced they are. So the face is not the most reliable source for detecting nonverbal "leakage" of deception cues.

Nor do the feet and legs offer much help. Feet are generally encased in shoes, and much of today's furniture is designed to shield the legs from view. Feet and leg motion, it is claimed, would offer more reliable cues since this kind of motion is usually not consciously monitored. But feet and legs are difficult to observe under normal circumstances.

That leaves the hands, and here, these researchers claim, is the richest field for the observation of deception cues. A gambler may be able to maintain a "poker" face when he is dealt a "royal flush," but he cannot easily control the excitement that manifests itself in the slight agitated movement of the small joints of the hands. Hands tremble, fingers drum, palms perspire, and arms move in spite of efforts at total control.

Teenage female students may offer an excellent

opportunity for observing the human hands in sub-conscious conversation. High school girls are, as they sometimes view it, competing for boys' attention and companionship. To attract boys many girls have learned a socially-accepted ritual that might be called "flirting behavior." Teachers certainly have many times observed these girls in action. But some girls, not wishing to appear so obvious about it, manage to maintain a controlled air of nonchalance. Whereas the open flirts will not hesitate to direct long glances at the boys of their choice, other girls seldom give more than passing glances. Flirts may tilt their heads to one side when appraising their "target" male, but covert flirts may control this behavior also. However, there are some accompanying hand motions the covert flirt is probably not conscious of, and which, if one is a careful observer, one may detect in spite of her efforts at control.

The first gesture is placing the hand on the hip when in the company of attractive males. This gesture is usually spontaneous, subconscious, and may occur many times during a period of contact. The second kind of gesture involves a variety of hand movements that frequently expose the front of the wrist and open palm. These movements may be quick and subtle, requiring a teacher's concentrated attention. But if he watches carefully, he may find the wrist and palm being turned toward the favored male whenever the male's glance is directed her way. Thus the controlled facial expressions of the covert flirt may not seem to express more than casual interest, but the hands say, "Come close to me."

Within the same context, the preening behavior of both male and female students is interesting to identify and observe. All animals seem to preen, but among humans preening occurs upon anticipated contact with the opposite sex. Some female students, for example, may verbally express little interest in males, but before entering a room where males are known to be present, they may stroke their hair, check their make-up, rearrange their clothes, and push their hair away from their eyes. Males may comb their hair, button their coats, and arrange their trousers. Even when in the company of other males and females, preening behavior may continue in spite of some students' apparent disinterest in the opposite sex. A young man, for example, may stand off by himself looking not the least interested in girls. But his preening behavior gives him away. It says, "Girls, look at me. I am attractive. I'm really interested in you. Please notice me." A sympathetic teacher just might be able to reduce some of the social stress in his classroom if he is able to detect these nonverbal cues at the outset.

Perhaps this is a good time to remind teachers once again that isolating single gestures for individual interpretation is seldom a valid proposition. The hair-patting and sweeping mentioned above is a good case in point. Hair-sweeping may be a preening gesture if all of the other components are present; on the other hand, hair-sweeping could be a totally defensive gesture. For example, women frequently groom their hair when they are agitated. If a female student does not agree with what others are saying or doing in a group discussion, this disagreement may manifest itself in excessive sweeping and patting of the hair. Male students often sweep back their hair when put on the defensive. A young man may voice a point of view or opinion that the group demonstrates to be incorrect or illogical. He may grudgingly give ground but as he does so, he may sweep his hair. When a male does something he believes to be wrong—crashing a lunch line or failing to observe a stop sign, for example,—the tendency is strong to sweep his hair. It is a defensive gesture that says, "So— I was wrong. What are you going to do about it?"

Thus, it is seldom fruitful to attach significant meaning to single, isolated gestures. They are best interpreted in context with other behavioral cues occurring in specific social settings. In fact, out of context, some gestures, such as those which accompany conversation, have little meaning at all.

For example, if a 16mm film of a group of people conversing is shown without the sound, one may notice all sorts of conversational gestures, but they have little meaning. When shown with the sound, however, the gestures take on more significance. One may notice that when a person asks a question, not only does his head move up at the end of the question, so do his hands. An observer must be alert to catch these small movements. If the scene has been filmed in close-up, one may also see the questioner's eyelids open wider.

Similarly, at the end of a statement, head, eyelids, and hands move down. Of themselves these gestures may go unnoticed. But when seen in conversational context, they become crucial to good order, because when a person moves neither up nor down, his listeners know that he wants to continue without interruption. These small gestures provide participants with cues for orderly social interaction, but when lifted out of a particular context, they may have no meaning at all.

Bilingual people who are at home with another language easily slip from one style of body language to the other. Teachers of foreign languages who stress only the verbal aspects of the language and neglect the significant body language cues that go along with conversation are missing a rare opportunity to steep their students in the new language. One of the most obvious shortcomings of today's language laboratories is that they are too highly word-oriented. It is not enough to listen to a language. One must watch it being spoken by experts to catch the body motion peculiar to the language. Even with films and videotape, however, a language teacher must help his students recognize and perform the appropriate body language if they are ever to feel comfortable with the new language.

As they move from their native tongue to a foreign language, particularly if the teacher insists on appropriate body motion, students may frequently "stutter" in body language. That is, a student may have to try the new motion again and again before he gets it right, and worse, he may mismatch his body cues so that he becomes thoroughly confused in both languages. No matter. This is the kind of learning that will stick to his bones. Many people after years of studying a foreign language never use it because they never really learned it in the first place. Like English grammar, foreign languages as they are taught in many schools are pale, one-dimensional ghosts of the living, dynamic systems of communication they are supposed to represent. A Frenchman not only speaks French, he thinks and moves in French. The French language is all of these, and it cannot be contained in a textbook or tape cassette.

Some gestures, because they occur so frequently and within full view, are easily observed. If a teacher introduces a touchy subject to a group of female students, many of them may demonstrate their uneasiness by crossing their arms over their chest. Sometimes only one student in the group will take offense, while the rest of the group or class will move right along with the discussion. Whether one or many, however, the teacher has an obligation to put his students at ease. When a teacher sees crossed arms and frequently crossed legs, he may wish to retreat from the offending topic or attempt to introduce it in a more agreeable fashion.

Hair-twirling is another easily observed gesture. When girls feel that the world is closing in on them and they wish they could return to the years of their childhood when mom and dad took care of everything, they may twirl their hair. Chronic hair-twirlers may need some help in facing up to the realities of life.

And of course there are the nail and cuticle biters. These are usually tense, up-tight students who would appreciate a little understanding from a teacher. It doesn't do much good to admonish them not to bite their nails. They don't enjoy it and would like to stop. A friendly relaxed classroom that doesn't contribute to their anxiety is more helpful than a thousand reprimands.

Sometimes, without meaning to, teachers make their students feel uneasy and inadequate. Students who wear eyeglasses may signal their distress by frequently removing and replacing their glasses, or they may cover their mouth under one guise or another. In either case, the message is plain, "You are making me feel uneasy and uncomfortable."

Agitation may also be readily observed. It usually begins with small finger movements, which are generally confined to the area within the silhouette of the body.

If the agitation continues to grow, the motion of the fingers grows. They may drum on the desk, tap with a pencil, or simply rub, scratch, or pick at the desk or clothing. Should the agitation grow into excitement, the motion will extend from the fingers to the larger joints of the wrist and arm and may move outside of the body silhouette.

In their book, *How to Read a Person Like a Book*, attorney Gerard Nierenberg and negotiating consultant Henry Calero have isolated and identified categories of gestures teachers might find useful in analyzing student behavior. The categories are:

Rejection gestures—Crossed arms or legs, tilting the head forward, moving the body backward, touching or rubbing the nose, rubbing the eye, or scratching behind the ear.

Readiness gestures—Hands on hips or hands on knees when seated, sitting on the edge of the chair, moving forward to speak confidentially.

Cooperation gestures—Sitting on the edge of the chair, putting the hand to the face, unbuttoning the coat or jacket, tilting the head.

Frustration gestures—Short breaths, patting the back of the neck, clenching hands, wringing hands.

Confidence gestures—Sitting up straight, maintaining eye contact, reducing eye blink, touching the finger tips of the hands together to form a steeple (and the more confidence, the higher the steeple!), elevating the feet on a desk or chair, touching or leaning against people or objects—a man may lean against *his* car or *his* wife to show ownership—elevating the body, leaning back with both hands supporting the head.

Nervous gestures—Clearing the throat, whistling, fidgeting.

Interrupt gestures—Raising the hand to the ear or lip, flicking up the hand.

Self-control gestures—Clenching the hands behind the back, locking the ankles when seated (as in dentist's chair), gripping the wrist.

Boredom gestures—Drumming the table, tapping the feet, clicking a ball point pen, holding the head in hands, doodling, staring blankly.

Acceptance gestures—Placing the hand to the chest, touching, moving closer.

Reassurance-seeking gestures—Clenching the hands and rubbing the thumbs together, pinching the hand or cuticle, placing pencil, pen, or paper clip in the mouth, touching the back of the chair before sitting, and, notably in women, placing the hand to the throat.

At the risk of unnecessary repetition, teachers must again be cautioned against lifting single, isolated gestures out of their behavioral matrix for interpretation. Everything should be considered—body movement, facial expression, verbalization, spatial cues, and the social setting in which all of these behaviors occur simultaneously. A teacher who is a skillful student of nonverbal communication may, with much practice, analyze a complete setting at a glance and arrive at a valid interpretation. Time and practice are necessary, but the results in understanding the behavior of students are well worth the effort. Attempting to assign meaning to single, isolated gestures is usually a fruitless, invalid activity.

Dances without Music

The legs and feet are possible sources of information but in the American culture they usually remain hidden or well covered. Shoes and stockings, trousers and skirts, the design of furniture, and even social custom make their observation difficult or impossible. Of course, some gestures are evident. Agitation that begins with toe tapping may grow into leg shaking and finally explode into kicking. Legs may cross at the ankles, which in context with other cues may signify mild negative feelings, or they may cross at the knees. Crossed knees and arms in females may signify deep personal aversion to ongoing events.

Researchers do not seem able at the moment to observe and identify significant, isolated leg and foot gestures. But some entire patterns of leg movement have been noted, and although information is sketchy and incomplete, a new avenue for investigation is within the realm of possibility. These patterns of leg movement have been called "dancing." They are sometimes so precise and predictable that they could be performed to music. There is the slow, rhythmic pacing of the hands-in-pockets walker—secretive and critical, the sort of person who enjoys putting other people down. Then there is the rapid, arms-free-and-swinging walker, a goal-oriented fellow who believes that a straight line is the shortest distance between two points. The prima donna of the rhythmic walkers is the hands-on-hips sprinter who moves in sudden bursts of energy, driven by the beat of his own secret drummer.

Observing dancing in the animal world has long been a favorite subject of investigators. Usually these dances are a part of a courtship ritual and are performed with all the pomp and circumstance of a formal dress ball. Even insects dance. The cautious male spider, driven by instincts beyond our comprehension, approaches the web of his predatory mate. Delicately he taps out a message on the outer strands of her web. If she is interested, she gently taps back. If she is not, she vigorously shakes the web, and one can imagine that the male loses little time in vacating the premises. So precariously balanced is the natural order that if the female spider chose to engage in deceptive behavior at these times, some species of spiders would shortly disappear.

Not so precarious, but just as precise, is the courtship dance of the American adolescent. In his book *Kinesics and Context* anthropologist Ray Birdwhistell cites a study of adolescent courtship undertaken some years ago at the University of Louisville. Of course it is possible that the "new morality" has rendered the results obsolete, and in that case the study must be repeated. But the ritual, as it was performed in the early sixties, had a coercive order that moved forward in time. There were twenty-four different steps, each performed in definite order and consisting of certain motions and signals that had to be learned. There were moves and countermoves throughout the sequence, with the male originating each new move and the female countering with the appropriate signal.

So standardized were these moves that the male usually would not move on to the next step until the female countered the previous move. For example, one of the original moves called for the boy to take the girl's hand. Assuming that he did so, he had to wait for the appropriate counter move—the girl must squeeze his hand. Then he was free to move on to the next step, the intertwining of fingers.

There was no agreed upon time limit for the completion of the dance. The entire twenty-four steps could take as little as one hour or as much as one year or more. Naturally, as with every lawful order, there were people who refused to be constrained by the order. A boy or girl who was considered "fast" might skip entire sequences or reverse their order. Sometimes the girl, rather than the boy, originated the next move. She was really "fast"! Or sometimes the girl did not supply the countermove, or the boy, to the exasperation of the girl, did not or could not progress to the next move. In that case, he was considered "slow." Most adolescents mastered this intricate dance, however, and performed it according to their code.

Men and women dance, too. As they engage in conversation, patterns of hand, leg, and foot motions mark the participants' moves and counter moves. Women glide into the courtship ritual with a slow, rhythmic rolling of the pelvic section of the body, accompanied by graceful hand movements to arrange the hair or smooth the dress. Men respond with hair patting, tie straightening, trouser and belt arranging, and checking the fingernails. If seated, women may then begin to cross and uncross their legs while their hands move delicately to the inside of calf, knee, or thigh. The heel of one shoe may be gracefully poised on the toe of the other. If filmed in slow motion, the entire sequence would take on the appearance of a slow, courtly dance whose steps are as rhythmical and predictable as a minuet. Men also "dance" with other men, but these steps seem to be more of a contest to determine status and dominance.

Recently, psychiatrists and clinical psychologists have been urged to observe the dances of their patients for diagnostic information. For example, a depressed patient may walk slowly without swinging his arms. If he is asked to walk across the room and turn, he may "block" turn. Most people, when turning, rotate their shoulders and head independently. But the depressed patient is more rigid. He turns as though his head and shoulders were one single unit.

So in spite of the customary attempts to conceal them, legs are beginning to provide new information about human behavior. Hopefully, alert, interested teachers will assist in this new study by becoming sensitized to the leg and foot motions of students as a possible source of information and by learning to devise procedures to identify, classify, and interpret the movements they observe.

A Nod of the Head

If they think of head-nodding as a message-sending procedure at all, most people are not usually impressed with its effectiveness or efficiency. This is because nods are frequently barely discernible and occur almost below the threshold of awareness. The nonverbal "yes" and "no" movements of the head are, of course, usually deliberate and intentional. Beyond these, however, most people fail to appreciate the role nodding plays in social interaction.

Suppose for a moment that a teacher is engaged in

conversation with a student. Single nods interspersed throughout the conversation may encourage the student to keep on talking. The teacher need not say a word. If he simply nods his head once in a while, the student will sustain most of the conversation.

Now suppose that the student says something requiring further elaboration. The teacher could verbally ask for elaboration, but many times two head nods will serve the same purpose. Or if a teacher is running a little late and he wishes to transmit the urgency of the situation to a student, two head nods may speed up the student's rate of delivery.

Suppose a teacher has been listening for some time and thinks the student has exhausted the possibilities of that particular subject or suppose he does not wish to talk about the subject at all. He wants the conversation to take a new direction. Three or more nods may encourage a change of subject or at least a fadeaway on the part of the speaker. The teacher must time these nods exactly right, however, or the result may not be what he wants. If his nods are not at least four-tenths of a second(!) in duration, the student may abruptly stop talking and ask him what is the matter.

Thus head nodding adds still another dimension to human communication. Many guidance counselors have incorporated head-nodding into their counseling procedure. They should realize, however, that nodding is not a neutral, objective motion. Rather, it is a positive, subjective procedure that encourages students to keep talking.

There are also some insidious aspects of head-nodding about which counselors ought to know. One may assert his dominance or superiority over another person by nodding his head in benign approval as another person talks. If the head-nodder continues his pattern of approval and the subordinate person is reduced to the level of seeking approval in the form of nodding, a pattern of superiority-inferiority may be established. Thus it is possible for a student to leave a counseling session feeling much inferior to the counselor, which is not the purpose at all.

Teachers are themselves frequently patronized in this fashion by supervisory personnel. Teachers, in turn, may patronize their students, and parents their own children. There is nothing wrong with occasional supportive nods as one is addressed by other people. In fact, nods encourage others to say what is on their minds. Patronizing in the form of prolonged silence accompanied by head-nodding is another matter.

Often people in authority come to expect subordinates to behave as inferiors. Teachers, for example, may expect students to continue talking when they nod their head. Sometimes, however, students refuse to follow this customary low status pattern, and teachers are left with the vague, uneasy feeling that students do not respect them. Neither teachers nor students, of course, are generally aware of the significance of head-nodding in these encounters. The behavior is usually subconscious. The feelings aroused, however, are conscious and real and will affect human relations in the classroom.

In their dealings with colleagues and superiors, teachers may find themselves being patronized by benign head-nodders. If they possess a wry sense of humor, they may be able to turn the situation around. All that is necessary is to get the other person to talk while teachers nod their heads in benign approval.

FOR FURTHER READING

Ardrey, Robert. *The Social Contract.* New York: Atheneum, 1970.

Birdwhistell, Ray L. *Kinesics and Context.* University of Pennsylvania Press, 1970.

Cameron, D. Ewen, M.D. "By sign and Shift, Tone and Tremor-Your Patient Talks." *Consultant,* vol. 6, no. 3, March, 1966, pp. 47–8.

Dudek, Stephanie Z. "Portrait of the Artist as a Rorschach Reader." *Psychology Today,* vol. 4, no. 12, May, 1971, pp. 46–50.

Ekman, Paul, and Wallace V. Friesen. "Nonverbal Leakage and Clues to Deception." *Psychiatry,* vol. 32, no. 1, 1969, pp. 88–106.

Fast, Julius. *Body Language.* New York: Evans, 1970.

Goffman, Erving. *Strategic Interaction.* Philadelphia: University of Pennsylvania Press, 1969.

Margoshes, Adam, and Collins, Glenn. "Right Handedness as a Function of Maternal Heartbeat." *Perceptual and Motor Skills,* vol. 20, 1965, pp. 443–4.

Mehrabian, Albert. "Communication without words." *Psychology Today,* Sept. 1968, vol. 2, no. 4, pp. 53–5.

Merle, Robert. *The Day of the Dolphin.* Greenwich, Conn.: Fawcett, 1970.

Nierenberg, Gerard I., and Calero, Henry. *How to Read a Person Like a Book.* New York: Hawthorn, 1971.

THE LANGUAGE
OF TOUCH

When life begins, the skin is already at work enfolding, wrapping, and sealing off a speck of life from everything else in the universe. Henceforth, the skin will mark the boundary of "self" and "not self," a living wall, paper thin, between a vulnerable organism and alien forces impinging upon it.

There is a general embryological law that states that the earlier a function develops, the more fundamental that function is likely to be. Thus, the skin is the most basic of organs for it makes possible the development of touch, the "mother of all the senses." As far as is known, touch is the earliest sensation to develop in the human embryo. With the development of touch awakens an awareness of a world beyond "self." The skin, a warm, pliable mantle to rub against the universe, is a most marvelous instrument for collecting "touch" data.

Most of what is known about the skin has been learned in recent times. This includes such information as how the skin behaves under different conditions and how it does what it is supposed to do. Much remains to be discovered.

If a person is of average size, he is wrapped in about sixteen to twenty square feet of skin. The largest of all the body organs, the skin weighs approximately six pounds. Although it is itself sixty percent liquid, the skin is nearly waterproof, a condition most appreciated when bathing or swimming. Unlike man-made waterproof containers, the skin not only repairs and regenerates itself but does so quickly and efficiently. Further, it is receptive to grafts, making possible large scale replacements where extensive areas have been destroyed.

To emphasize the toughness and durability of the skin, at no point is it more than three-sixteenths of an inch thick. In fact, when a person walks barefoot across a lawn or along a pebbly beach, just one-sixteenth of an inch of skin separates him from injury. While he sleeps, a mere one five-hundredth of an inch is sufficient to protect his delicate eyeballs from all sorts of painful possibilities.

Unfortunately, the thickness of the skin does not remain constant during one's lifetime. Skin thickness declines by approximately one half between the ages of twenty and eighty. This explains why the skin of elderly people is so delicately fragile. Designers of clothing, including footwear, for the elderly should take this information into account. Even ordinary household utensils and appliances, which pose few problems for the young and middle-aged, present many difficulties for the aged.

Further, the resiliency of the skin also declines with age and by sex. Evidently men have more supple skin than women. It wears better with the passage of years. Some men manage to maintain youthful-looking skin well into middle age and beyond. Women seldom do. Women, however, receive compensation of another order. The female of all ages is more responsive to tactile stimuli.

Perhaps one answer to skin durability lies in genetic engineering. When mechanical harvesting devices for tomatoes came into general use some years ago, they bruised and destroyed many tomatoes during the harvesting process. One solution, of course, was to discontinue the use of harvesting machinery. Agriculturists, however, sought another answer to the problem. Tomato growers "engineered" a new kind of tomato with a thicker skin that was less susceptible to damage. At the present time, the basic, spherical shape of the tomato still poses problems for mechanical packing equipment. Is a cube-shaped tomato on the way? Or thick-skinned people?

The skin is a round-the-clock guardian. It never sleeps. Over half a billion sensory fibres shuttle messages back and forth from the skin to body control centers, regulating heat, moisture, and pressure and performing hundreds of routine adjustments. Feedback is continuous. Silently, efficiently, the skin works on and on, one of the most sensitive and durable wrappers in nature.

Basically, the skin performs four functions: (1) It protects the underlying parts from injury and invasion. (2) It is a temperature regulator. By exposing a large surface to the surrounding air, it permits the rapid dissipation of internal heat build-up. Consequently, the more skin surface exposed, the more rapid the cooling process. Although most teachers are familiar with this simple principle of thermodynamics, some fail to recognize it in operation in the classroom. Small children, for example, do not possess the same square footage of skin as adults. Thus they retain more heat. First-graders generally feel warmer than their teacher. Add to this the constant heat-generating movements of young children, and one will realize that there is a significant difference between students' idea of a comfortable temperature and the teacher's.

Since a few degrees either way can seriously affect the amount and quality of human work, proper temperature regulation becomes an important variable in the design of work environments. Perhaps in the future, temperature regulation will be computerized and the temperature will be matched to the on-going activities of the classroom. Meanwhile, another dimension may be added to "dedication" of teachers. In a previous chapter it was suggested that dedication means dressing and decorating in colors most appealing to the students, not to the teacher. Now it is suggested that dedication also means wearing a jacket or sweater to class and adjusting the thermostat for the comfort of students.

(3) The third function of the skin is to act as a metabolic organ. Although it is seldom popular to speak of the body as a machine, the analogy is not only valid but obvious. A machine is designed to do work. How does it get the energy to do the work? By "metabolizing" fuel of some sort. An automobile acquires energy by "metabolizing" gasoline, that is, by releasing the energy stored in raw fuel and applying it to the wheels of the car through a drive chain. Unneeded gasoline is stored in the fuel tank. Other devices, such as the manifold,

muffler, and tail pipe, assist in the "metabolic" process by venting to the outside environment such unneeded by-products as heat, noise, and fumes.

As the human body metabolizes food for energy, the skin stores excess fuel in the form of fat, a reminder to match food consumption to the expenditure of energy or suffer the consequences of metabolic imbalances. The skin also vents to the outside excess water and salt in the form of perspiration—which suggests a careful consideration of current chemicals to prevent perspiration. After all, wastes cannot be utilized by or contained indefinitely within a well-functioning machine of any kind.

(4) The fourth function of the skin is the one of central concern in this chapter—the skin as a sense organ. Should there remain any doubt as to the importance of the skin in this regard, a disproportionately large area of the cortex of the brain is charged with the exclusive responsibility of monitoring tactile information. This kind of data is so important to the well-being of the whole body that in the busy, crowded crevices and folds of the cortex, information about what is being "felt" at any moment is given top priority.

If not consciously, then at least subconsciously, people all over the world seem to suspect that information picked up by the skin is highly personal and full of deep meaning. They react in different ways. Some cover the skin completely, even when temperature and climatic conditions make covering unnecessary. Others uncover the skin completely to "feel" as much as possible. And still others cover some parts and not others to arrive at an accommodation between the conventional and the "natural." Groups of serious people gather to touch and to send and receive "vibrations" through skin contact. "Touch" is a magic word today, offered as a shortcut to improved family life or race relations. The skin has become a focus for cultism, fetishism, mysticism, and other assorted practices. What is fact and what is fiction? The truth is, the skin is full of surprises, and while a sort of mythology has grown up around touch, some genuine findings in recent years pose possibilities and implications unknown just a short time ago. This newer information will form the basis of the following discussion.

A Loving Touch

Who will deny the power or popularity of love? But who will define it? Yet until love is defined, intelligent discourse on the subject is almost impossible. Love as a private, personal experience is beyond investigation, beyond description except in the most general terms, and even then, usually by example and through inference. No one is surprised that children who are loved by their parents usually do better in school than children who are not. But what does love do and how does it do it? Until these questions are answered in some observable, rational way, "love" is just a sound made by the vocal apparatus. If love is such a powerful agency of human development and humane existance, it must have an objective reality that can be investigated, analyzed, and defined.

If this approach to love seems sterile to teachers, they are indulging in a luxury not permitted serious students of communication—they have closed their minds to a subject whose limits are unknown. Love is love, they may say, and it cannot be described or defined, studied or analyzed. But perhaps ancient people felt the same way about thunder and lightning. Today, however, having studied and analyzed the powerful forces involved in storms, human beings respect such natural phenomena in ways that transcend the primitive fears and superstitions of their forebears. Perhaps one day, having analyzed the mysterious phenomenon called "love," other humans will come to experience it in a more objective, rational way. Meanwhile, the first glimmerings of understanding are at hand.

Love is touching. In his book, *Touching: The Human Significance of the Skin*, Ashley Montagu summarizes much of what is now known about the skin and its relationship to human development. Montagu notes that if there is one observation common to most investigations into the behavior of animals and their young it is this: handling during the early days of life results in significantly greater increases in weight, more activity, less fearfulness, greater ability to withstand stress, and greater immunity to disease. Rats, for example, who are handled during the first ten days of life usually weigh more, learn better, and survive longer than rats who are not.

Love increases an animal's chances for survival. Animals who are not loved, that is, not touched or handled, are, from the first moments of life, disadvantaged.

Nor is love a one-way process. The benefits to the one who loves are sometimes as great as those received by the ones loved. In dogs, for example, the rooting, nuzzling, and nursing of young pups help the mother to recover from the ordeal of giving birth. Because of this, Montagu suggests that the routine separation of human mother and infant needs serious reconsideration. In the name of sterile procedures and good administrative practice, some maternity hospitals still deny the new mother what might well be the most potent instrument of recovery—her own child.

From this point of view, then, love becomes less mysterious but not less necessary for healthy development. In fact, the more one is able to understand the unique physiological contributions made by love to a developing organism, the more one comprehends and appreciates in a profound and rational way the complexity of life.

Love may also be approached from another tactile direction. Love is licking. All animals, with the exception of human females and the great apes, lick their new-born. Most people have undoubtedly witnessed this phenomenon more than a few times. At first glance one is struck by the meticulous care lavished by the mother on the young. Endlessly, she grooms and cleans them, gently but thoroughly. She loves them.

If one regards love as a mysterious, unknown, and unknowable power, one might be tempted to end the matter here. But if two important questions are asked —"What does love do and how?"—a whole new avenue of intellectual adventure opens up. Careful observation of animal mothers will reveal that the rate and region of licking are seldom random. The mother follows a program of licking so precise and predictable that she may be timed with a stopwatch. Mother cats, for example, deliver three to four licks per second. The most licking occurs in the genital and perineal region, then in the mouth region, the underbelly, and the back and sides, all exactly in that order.

If love is licking and licking is crucial to healthy

development, what does licking do? If one answers, licking grooms and cleans, he is only partially right. Actually, he is wrong, for that is not the function of licking at all, even though cleanliness occurs as a consequence. The key to the riddle is to observe where most of the licking takes place—in the perineal region between the external genitalea and the anus. In the early stages of life the gastro-intestinal tract must be constantly stimulated into action, "primed" as it were, until the developing organs take this function upon themselves. Without the tactile stimulation of licking, elimination is difficult and sometimes impossible for newborn animals.

Breeders of chihauhau dogs, for example, noted that mothers made no attempts to lick their young. Many pups were lost for lack of love—licking!—until breeders undertook this chore themselves with cotton swabs.

Again the absolute necessity for the kind of behavior associated with love is evident. The point is, however, that until love is analyzed in terms of its unique contributions to survival, little of real value is known about it. Songwriters and poets may take for granted the power of love, but teachers may not. They must investigate it, for love or the lack of it impinges directly or indirectly on their work. This does not mean that the teacher's task is more important or more intellectually stimulating than the poet's. It is merely different.

Can the information about tactile stimulation gleaned from animal studies be generalized to the human situation? The evidence is steadily mounting that indeed it may. When a newborn infant is placed in direct contact with its mother, the swollen uterus of the mother is stimulated to contract. Immediate breast feeding also assists in uterine recovery. Further, breast feeding helps to detach the placenta and stimulates the contractions that lead to its ejection. As for the benefits to the infant, colostrum contained in the mother's milk, which lasts a mere two days or so, immunizes the baby against a number of diseases. And, of course, today's young mothers are familiar with the many studies supporting the belief that breast-fed children tend to be mentally and physically superior.

The life sciences are a long way from discovering how tactile communication operates, that is, the physiological nature of the stimulation, its transmission channels, the mechanisms that come into play, and their modes of operation. Nevertheless, a growing body of evidence supports the assumption that tactile stimulation is just as important to human infants as to all other animals.

But if licking is so important for animals, what substitutes for licking in the human experience? Dr. Montagu theorizes that the answer may be the uterine contractions of labor. As the uterus works to expel the fetus, its walls massage and stimulate the entire body of the fetus, preparing it to take up an existance of its own after birth. The fact is, humans are born immature and remain immature for a longer period of time than any other animal. The evidence would seem to indicate that humans simply are not ready for birth at the end of nine months. Uterine contractions merely begin a sensitizing process, which should be continued after birth if an infant is to develop normally.

This poses still another question. Why is the human fetus born at nine months? Wouldn't twelve or eighteen months in the comfortable, safe environment of the uterus be more advantageous? It would, except for one hard reality—because of the size of the human brain and its rapid growth, if a fetus were not born at nine months, it would be difficult, often impossible, for it to be born at all. So nature has reached a compromise. The immature fetus is given a massive skin massage and expelled while head size is still manageable, but the job of sensitizing must be continued by the mother long after birth. The brain, of course, continues to grow rapidly. (At the end of three years, the human child has attained ninety percent of its full brain growth.)

There remains one final point on the importance of skin stimulation to human babies. Caesarean-delivered babies are denied uterine stimulation, and its absence should be detectable in important life functions. Such indeed seems to be the case. Montagu notes that the mortality rate of infants so delivered is two to three times as high as vaginal-delivered babies. Caesarean babies also exhibit greater lethargy, decreased reactivity, and cry less frequently. In later years they tend toward speech defects, fear of school, personality difficulties, restlessness, and temper tantrums.

Thus many of the behaviors associated with loving, especially tactile stimulation, have their bases in animal physiology. Love is utilitarian. It sustains and supports basic life processes. Love may be biochemical, physiological, kinesic, tactile, auditory, and visual. Love takes many forms. Not to be loved is to be denied these therapeutic sensations. When such deprivation occurs at the very onset of life, all animals, including humans, suffer consequences from which complete recovery is just about impossible. Without love, the quality and sometimes the quantity of life is forever diminished.

So a "loving touch" is indeed a reality, so necessary

for healthy development that the where, when, and how long to touch has been genetically programmed into the maternal behavior of most animals. Far from diminishing the worth of love, recent studies demonstrate beyond the shadow of a doubt that the cluster of behaviors associated with love are at the very core of survival.

When People Touch

As far back as ancient Babylon a ritualistic "laying on of hands" has been recorded. The practice is probably just as common today. Is it possible that through thousands of years of human experience so many people could have been wrong? Or does the touch of a hand actually transmit messages and meanings that transcend the human capacity to decode and describe them conciously? Perhaps.

What is lacking, however, is conclusive evidence. Without dealing in mysticism or other supersensory practices, how does one go about designing research to demonstrate the reality of tactile message sending and receiving? Probably even more basic, is it possible to attract respectable scientists to a field so overrun with mystics, amateur zealots, and assorted charlatans? As a group, scientists are rather cautious and highly sensitive to the criticism of their peers. They tend to write for and speak to their own kind rather than to ordinary people. Of course, there are notable exceptions. But it will take men and women of science who are secure and confident in the management of their sciences to break this new and difficult ground. Look for some startling advances, however, in the decades of the seventies and eighties, because there are unexplained and documented phenomena that intelligent, curious scholars cannot ignore. Putting one's arm around the victim of an asthmatic attack, for example, will more than likely alleviate the attack or halt it altogether. Workers in homes for the aged, hospitals, and nursery schools have noted that nothing soothes the old, the sick, the very young, and the distressed like the touch of a sympathetic human. Infants reach out for adults, and adults reach out toward each other and the universe. What kind of information do humans gather through touch? How is it processed? How is it used? What does it mean? Answers are meager and inadequate.

The human female, as has been noted previously, responds more readily to tactile stimuli than the male. Males, by the way, respond better to visual stimuli. The high receptivity of the female to touch may be learned rather than "wired-in." In American culture, for example, girls are permitted more tactile expressions of affection than boys. Mothers seem happier to have girls, and, as a rule, girls tend to be weaned later than boys. So it is difficult to determine at the present time if males are tactically disadvantaged by culture or by nature. At any rate, the male's reduced receptivity to touch is just one more example of the confusing role thrust upon the male in American culture. On the one hand he is taught (largely by females) to reject all overt displays of affection. Try to find a fifth-grade boy who enjoys being hugged and kissed by anybody, for example. But on the other hand, if he learns his cultural lessons well, he is accused (again, largely by females) of being aggressive, unsensitive, and domineering. Further, the unnatural behaviors thrust upon the male take their toll in reduced life span and in many physical disorders and aberrations.

Lack of tactile stimulation as well as deep feelings of frustration, rage, and guilt in both males and females may result in excessive scratching. Rocking, too, is another form of substitute satisfaction of the need for passive-movement stimulation. Normally the mother satisfies this need. But large families or busy or disinterested mothers frequently allow needs to go unattended. Self-rocking may result. Rocking, by the way, merits a closer look.

Rocking produces a gentle stimulation of all areas of the skin. There are those who argue that the cradle should never have been discarded, since it admirably served this purpose. The crib is merely a rigid slab, unresponsive and unmoving. Cribs with bars are cold, lonely cages, removed from the mainstream of family life, and here most children spend the first and most important year of their lives in deadening isolation. A much better place for a baby is the kind of nylon sling worn today by some young mothers. The baby is always in contact with its mother's body, rocked by her movements, comforted by her presence. Slings are inconvenient, of course, and undoubtedly tiring for the mother, so the baby sling will probably never become popular with most American mothers. But mothers' freedom will be bought at the expense of the kinds of children who emerge from lonely cribs and nurseries at the end of one or two years.

There is evidence that babies who are rocked gain more weight. Again, the therapeutic components of rocking and their modes of operation are unexplained except in the vaguest of inferences. It is known that mothers who rock their babies tend to synchronize the rhythm of the rocking with either the mother's or the baby's respiratory rate. However, the gentle patting of babies tends to synchronize with the heartbeat. Rocking and patting are soothing to babies because they are outward reinforcements of natural, inward rhythms. But what does it all mean?

Teachers who have chaperoned school dances in recent years have undoubtedly noticed the almost complete absence of touch between the dancing couples. Instead, they face each other and simply rock and sway to the rhythm of the music. Young people call their music "rock," by the way. Are these young people the vanguard of the unrocked generations, the unfulfilled isolates of secluded cribs and nurseries? What are they trying to say, and what can be done about it?

Tactile Communication

In the late 1960's researchers at Princeton University's Cutaneous Communications Laboratory engaged in an interesting experiment. They attached small vibrators to various regions of the bodies of human subjects and activated them by remote transmitters. A code was devised, which the subjects learned. For example, the letter "W" might be represented by a buzz on the right shoulder, the right leg, the left leg, and the left shoulder in that order. By varying the intensity, duration, and pitch of the vibrations, additional information could be coded. Once they learned the code, subjects were able to detect and respond to signals sent from remote stations. In effect, the human body became a receiver of coded information sent across distances.

This kind of skin communication is feasible because the skin has hundreds of thousands of "tactile receptors" capable of detecting and discriminating among various degrees of pressure, pain, stroking, tickling, and so forth. The skin, in fact, is so highly sensitive that phone conversations have been converted into vibrations which, when applied directly to the skin, have enabled subjects after just a few hours of practice to understand complete spoken sentences. In this case the skin was made to vibrate just like the speaker of a telephone, radio, or hi-fi set. Human subjects learned to associate certain kinds of vibrations with specific words. After learning to detect single words, subjects were taught to "feel" word chains and finally to recognize complete sentences.

It is difficult to determine exactly where and how these new techniques may be used to best advantage. Certainly there is a whole new range of uses in treating hearing disabilities. There may also be some imminent breakthroughs in such difficult fields of study as underwater communication. If past experience is much of a guide for predicting future use, however, the most practical applications are simply beyond the edge of the imagination at present. Thomas Edison thought his motion picture projector would be used as an educational tool. He never dreamed of film as an entertainment medium, so he did not take out a European patent on his device. It is fatuous to condemn his lack of vision. The cinema was simply beyond imagination at that time. Similarly, the idea of skin communication is so new that it is difficult to predict its future beyond the range of today's limited experience.

Tactile communication is common to many other animals. In fact, some animals use it to better advantage than humans. Robert Froman points out some interesting examples in his book, *The Great Reaching Out: How Living Beings Communicate.* Rattlesnakes, for example, are susceptible to their own venom. Consequently when they engage in combative behaviors, they dare not bite each other. They meet chest to chest and shove. The winner simply out-shoves the loser, who retires to regain his dignity. He will return to shove again another day. If humans would accept a "shoving ritual" in place of more violent measures, they could spare each other much pain and bloodshed. Young boys seem to understand the ritual better than adults. They meet and push. The more aggressive youngster pushes harder. The less aggressive lad usually gets the message—he must push still harder or quit. Unless a crowd has gathered and is screaming for blood, he usually offers token resistance and retires. This sort of male combat barely receives a passing glance in most animal species —it is too common and of little importance. Why violence is so fascinating to humans is an intriguing riddle.

Skin pressure also establishes dominance in lizards. They meet, forehead to forehead, and shove. Cows are a little more subtle. They push sideways. And chickens peck. All are using a deep sense of pressure to establish their place in the social hierarchy.

Some animals use pressure for gentler purposes. The massive trunk of the elephant can become a delicate, feeling extension to explore unknown things. Prairie dogs and manatees "kiss." All cats, tigers and toms, lick. Gentle pressure sometimes works wonders. Hand-milked cows give more and richer milk than those milked by machine.

But perhaps the most startling news of all in recent

years is in an area which, for want of a better name, might be called "plant psychology." An old Chinese proverb states, "The best fertilizer for a plant is its owner's shadow." Interest in this field of study goes back to 1966 when quite by accident Cleve Backster, a polygraph (lie detector) operator, attached his instrument to a green plant. The curious Mr. Backster was not prepared for what followed.

The plant registered "emotion." The stylus of the polygraph fluctuated as though it were recording human emotions. The plant responded to human thoughts, especially when they concerned threats to the plant's safety. Most reputable scientists were disinclined to take this incredible news seriously. One intrepid researcher, psychiatrist Aristide Esser of Rockland State Hospital, New York, however, repeated the procedure and obtained similar results.

Now the curiosity of Dr. J. B. Rhine of ESP fame has been piqued. He saw in plant communication a new avenue for research in a field closely related to extrasensory perception. Thus far, Rhine's "green thumb" studies show that plants do grow better for some people than for others. Which people? People who "love" their plants? Biochemist Bernard Grad of McGill University in Montreal determined that a noted faith healer released a measurable flow of energy to plants when he touched them. Incredible as it may seem, the evidence does indicate that under certain conditions plants seem to respond both to human thoughts and human touch.

These studies in plant psychology certainly raise more questions than they answer. They are controversial, of course, and most reputable scientists approach them, if at all, with deep skepticism. But then the earth was around long before science acknowledged it. Plants are living matter. They metabolize food, grow, move, and respond to forces in the universe far beyond our inadequate resources to describe and catalog. Plants inhabited the earth eons before humans and other living species. They have survived and flourished. Without the green plants of earth to replenish the oxygen content of the atmosphere, all forms of terrestrial life, with the exception of some bacteria, would soon disappear. Why, then, need we deny plants the ability to communicate?

If nothing else, the teacher has a new avenue of exploration and discovery. In this age of complicated technology, what better way to keep perspective than to gain new insights into the ways and wonders of the green life that springs directly from the earth. Posters reminding and admonishing students to keep the earth green may serve some useful purpose. But the real issue is to understand the ecosystem called "life." The faintest glimmer of understanding how one kind of life runs into another and how all intermingle into a kaleidoscopic whole is worth a thousand posters.

When Teachers Touch

Like medicine, teaching should be a touching profession. Within arm's length are the young, healthy, and curious, reaching out to be touched by the teacher. If after a few years in school many children have withdrawn unfulfilled, then it is time to examine seriously the joyless system that suffocates the young in their academic cradles. Certainly they enter school eager enough. From rich homes and poor, from all stages and walks of life, the young pour into America's schools. To go to a real school, to learn real things, to touch and be touched by a real, live teacher—have you forgotten how it was?

But soon the suffocation begins. Eyes and ears are clogged with meaningless information while hands lie idle. The whole universe is funneled through books and the words of teachers. Bright children who had rolled in learning, rubbed it on, tasted it, smelled it, covered themselves with it, suddenly find themselves lost, bewildered, and unused. Out of the crunch of time and numbers, regimentation and abstraction, are born the misfits and deviants who will never fit the system and whom the system will never fit.

Only the teacher can humanize this process and salvage the lost and the disillusioned. Where is the teacher who will move among students as a helper and not a judge, as a friend and not an enforcer? The '70s and the '80s, and perhaps the whole future, belong to him. More and more as sophisticated packages of learning materials and procedures becomes available and communication technology takes over routine drill and instruction, the teacher's task will change. No longer a dispenser of information, a drill master, and judge, the new teacher will be a humanizer, a buffer between the child and the system. The new teacher will fit the system to the child.

Certainly this will not happen tomorrow, but it will happen sooner than teachers think. Tomorrow, however, is not too soon to begin the humanizing process. And begin it, where possible, by touching students, especially if one teaches small children. An encouraging pat or a sympathetic arm around the shoulders when students are discouraged or distressed may work small wonders. It is a fact—a measurable flow of electrical energy passes from one person to another during tactile stimulation. Although the origins and meaning of this energy are not clear, its presence is evident, and its effect on human behavior is beyond dispute. A sympathetic human touch soothes the sick and the distressed, the very young, and the very old. Do not underestimate the power of touch.

If a teacher is not a "toucher," however, any sudden change in his behavior could do more harm than good. Most students learn to expect a certain kind of behavior from a teacher. To change suddenly will upset them. One might begin by talking gently, working forward by performing simple acts—shaking hands or patting on the shoulder. Give students time to become accustomed to the new approach. Above all, a teacher should be emotionally honest. Touch should not be used to manipulate, dominate, or deceive young people.

Unfortunately, in our culture male teachers are not permitted the latitude of touching allowed to female teachers. Some communities are more permissive than others, but the male teacher must ever be on the alert not to offend community mores. Lives and careers have been ruined by over-stepping the touch limits of the community. In one of its final issues, *Look* magazine documented the story of a male teacher whose friendship with his young students evidently went beyond community mores. Although he was ultimately cleared of all charges, the teacher left the community sadder but wiser, and the children lost a good friend.

Even though information is sketchy and disjointed, enough has been learned about tactile communication in recent years to warrant serious investigation by researchers in many fields. While sensitivity groups dedicated to a reawakening of body awareness may serve some useful purpose in alerting people to a neglected world of tactile stimulation, long-range benefit will come about only through systematic study. Teachers have much to gain by keeping informed of new developments. Perhaps as important, here is a field to which teachers can make a significant contribution. Machines can do marvelous things to assist with routine instruction, but only a teacher can touch. Only a teacher can wipe away tears, hold small hands, and hug children who have tried hard.

FOR FURTHER READING

Boulton, Brett. "Do Plants Think?" *Ladies Home Journal,* October 1970, p. Tb.

Froman, Robert. *The Great Reaching Out: How Living Beings Communicate.* Cleveland: World, 1968.

Geldard, Frank A. "Body English." *Psychology Today,* vol. 2, no. 7, Dec. 1968, pp. 43–7.

Howard, Jane. *Please Touch.* New York: McGraw-Hill, 1970.

Kaiser, Robert Blair. "What Happened to a Teacher Who Touched Kids." *Look,* August 10, 1971, pp. 64–8.

McMahon, Edwin M., and Peter A. Campbell. *Please Touch* (Search Book). New York: Sheed and Ward, 1969, pp., photos.

Montagu, Ashley. *Touching: The Human Significance of the Skin.* New York: Columbia University Press, 1970.

Nourse, Alan E. *The Body.* New York: Time Life, 1964.

TIME AND
OTHER WONDERS

Time is a language. Suppose a student makes an appointment to see a teacher at 3:30 p.m. When he arrives promptly, he finds the teacher already waiting for him. The teacher has used time to tell the student that he is eager to see him, so eager, in fact, that he came early. The student has used time to show the teacher that he is punctual and reliable. If either one had been late for the appointment—for whatever reason —a different kind of message would have passed between them.

Sometimes time contradicts other languages. An elementary school teacher may tell his students that arithmetic is just as important as history, yet he devotes more time to history. His students know which subject the teacher thinks is more important. Or school authorities may try to impress students with the importance of good eating habits and then give them thirty minutes for lunch (ten minutes of which are spent waiting on line). Or the school principal may tell his faculty that he is sincerely interested in their problems, yet he spends most of the day in his office.

The use of time as a medium of communication is culture-based. In American culture, for example, an executive expects not to be kept waiting when he arrives on time to confer with another busy executive. But if he makes an appointment with an executive in Hong Kong or Tokyo, he can expect to cool his heels in an outer office for thirty minutes or more. If the American does not understand how the Oriental uses time, he might feel insulted. To an Oriental, however, the delay is customary. An Oriental businessman expects to wait a prescribed time when he visits an American executive. If he is ushered in immediately upon arrival, and if he does not understand American use of time, he is liable to be suspicious and confused.

Even within the same culture, time is used differently. People in the large urban areas of the northeastern United States always seem to be in a hurry. When they drive South for vacation, they are frequently exasperated by the loose sense of time of Southerners. They expect waitresses in restaurants to work as fast as their counterparts in New York City. But waitresses in Mobile work to the beat of a different drummer. There is a world of difference between a "New York second" and a "Mobile second." If the Northern tourist does not adapt to the local rhythm, his Southern vacation could be a distressing experience.

Time is an elusive variable for serious study because it is undefinable. To the psychologist time is a dimension of consciousness. To the physicist time is one of the three basic quantities (the other two are mass and distance) by which he can describe anything in the universe. To the teacher time is a schedule of activities. In truth, time as we know and measure it is beyond definition. In space, for example, where distance is measured in light years and events happen in milleseconds, hours and days have little meaning.

To the teacher whose work begins and ends at the sound of a bell, and whose day is fragmented into precise intervals timed by automatic clocks, speculation on the meaning and nature of time is purely academic. Yet a teacher is often a slave of time precisely for the reason that teachers have not examined the concept of time foisted on them and their students by tradition. Flexible scheduling may offer some relief from the tyranny of time, but the problem is much more complicated. The mechanical timing of students for whatever reason needs thoughtful review. The school year is divided into semesters or quarters, the quarters into days, the days into periods, the periods into sub-periods. Why? Somewhere along the way education has been confused with time serving.

One of the blights of the Industrial Revolution, which permeated the nineteenth century and persisted into the twentieth century, was the mechanical timing of human beings. In the 1930s industry attempted to improve productivity through time and motion studies. A skilled workman was timed as he performed a certain task. He set the criterion every one was supposed to meet. Industrial psychologists, however, did not reckon with the quirks and kinks of human behavior. When the time-and-motion man was in the vicinity, the model worker merely worked slower. In some cases, an entire assembly line slowed down regardless of the example set by the criterion. The result in many cases was exactly the opposite to that sought by industrial managers—productivity dropped. Time and motion studies were abandoned.

Public education as a precisely timed process is a product of nineteenth century thought. Students cannot and will not become productive on and off on cue, nor can everyone be expected to match some artificial criterion of efficiency. If they are forced into a mechanical production line, students will emulate workers of an earlier day who were caught in the same sort of dehumanizing grind. They will sabotage and cheat because the alternative is unendurable to them. Regularly scheduled examinations, midterm and final exams, and weekly progress tests that all students must take at exactly the same time are examples of the mechanical production-line concept. Every teacher must surely know that students learn in different ways and at different rates. Yet all are tested at the same time and in the same way. When an examination means pass or failure, graduation or retention, can students really be faulted for trying to outwit a system that demonstrates so little regard for their welfare?

Time, as has been noted, is handled differently by different people. Undoubtedly teachers have known students who thrived on closely-timed schedules of activities. Just as surely they have also known students who panicked at deadlines. Isn't the answer obvious? People work best when they are permitted to set their own rhythms. True, this could play havoc with current administrative practices. In the long run, however, it will prove easier to change administrations than the genetic and culturally learned behavior of human beings.

In fact, no one knows at present just how to go about

changing the time perceptions of people. The ability to cope with time was thought to reside in the frontal lobes of the brain. Lobotomized monkeys, for example, frequently could not remember for more than a few seconds. More recent evidence points to the existence of a body "pacemaker" that governs perception of time and the infinity of behaviors associated with time. Its location, make-up, and mode of operation are profound mysteries, however. Humans are unique among animals because they possess a sense of present, past, and future. How they do it is the riddle.

If people handled time differently, would it not be possible to make predictions about their behavior based on a study of how they do perceive time? Some people "live in the past." Others "live in the future." And there are those who live "only for today." Each type has a pattern of behavior that is fairly predictable.

Past types are the souvenir collectors. They tend to be emotional and subjective. When confronted with problems in the present, frequently they look to the past for answers. Usually they have a strict moral code and tend toward conservatism. Punctuality is not one of their virtues.

Present types act on the spur of the moment. They are "now" oriented. They want to do something immediately. Delays annoy them. They don't believe in saving for a rainy day or waiting patiently for information they want right now.

Future types would rather deal with what is possible than with what exists at present. They inspire others with their ideas and their dreams. Before they work out the details of one dream, however, they are off on another.

There must be people with a balanced sense of time,

who manage to keep the past, present, and future in perspective. What of them? They, too, are a type. They will usually be found doing well in the sciences. They are able to grasp the "wholeness" of things. Unfortunately, they sometimes give the impression that they are cold, detached, and uncaring. But they are not. They are easy to identify. They ask lots of questions.

Human beings are finite creatures. They live and die in the short run. There are many times and many circumstances when measures of time are important. Time is easy to measure—it requires only a clock or a calendar. Learning is much more difficult to measure. Perhaps that is why some teachers choose to measure time rather than learning.

Anthropologist Ray Birdwhistell makes a useful distinction between "timing" and "clocking." Timing, he says, refers to events that occur in an explicitly defined sequence. For example, a music teacher might teach music reading by introducing the music staff, then note names, note values, and measure signatures exactly in that order. Timing is important. Clocking, on the other hand, refers to, as Birdwhistell puts it, "calendrical or horological frames"—days, hours, and minutes. One has little to do with the other. Timing would be similar for most students. Clocking would vary from student to student.

Birdwhistell's distinction may help teachers reorder their instructional patterns. Most teaching strategies would probably require timing, that is, a coersive order or sequence of events, each event building on the ones preceding and leading toward the events that follow. Few strategies would require the precise clocking of students. For the teacher, the challenge is to determine the timing sequence and the degree of clocking, if any.

But to confuse timing and clocking seems not to be sound educational practice.

Smell

Smell is not ordinarily thought of as a medium of communication, but it is—and a very potent one. For example, only within the last few decades has the complex social structure of communities of ants, bees, and termites been fully analyzed and appreciated. Such communities could not exist in their great complexity without elaborate language systems. And, at least in the case of social insects, smell is the base upon which language is built.

Information is coded in the form of *pheromones* that are "read" and interpreted by other members of the same species. A pheromone is just the opposite of a hormone. A hormone is a chemical that is secreted internally and controls internal functions. A pheromone is excreted into the outside environment and conveys information to other insects of the same species. Pheromonal communication is used by ants to lay food trails, by queen bees to control the sex drive of workers, and by termites for identification purposes.

Researchers in the field of pheromonal communication are convinced that pheromones are a dominant means of communication in many animal species, if not in most, including humans. For example, when a minnow is attacked, it gives off a chemical to warn other minnows in the vicinity. In this particular case the message is clearly related to species' survival and is so important that nature has encoded the alarm in a most explicit, way—an easily recognized scent.

One of the most frustrating exercises in the study of

human behavior, however, has been the search for human pheromónes. While researchers generally agree that humans do produce pheromones, none has been identified thus far. The odor-producing chemicals released by human males and females are essentially similar. Thus, unlike many other animal species, odor is not a constant gender marker among humans. But the search for human pheromones continues and in all probability will be rewarded in the future with some new information about intra-species behavior control via excreted chemicals.

If pheronomes are difficult to isolate and identify, however, ordinary scents and odors are commonplace. Many of these are excellent examples of inter-species communication based on smell. Camels, for example, have an effective way of dealing with annoying humans. They spit, and if that doesn't do the job, they may even add a little of their foul smelling stomach contents. Needless to say, it is an unusual camel driver who has been spat on twice by an irate camel. Toads are covered with an effective chemical repellent, as many puppies discover. And, of course, skunks move unmolested through a hostile world, their only defense being a strong odor that once experienced is forever remembered.

The power of smell should not be underrated. A pregnant mouse will abort at the first odor of a strange male. The reason seems simple enough. There aren't supposed to be strange males in the vicinity of pregnant mice. If there are, it means the population has gotten out of hand, and the last thing an over-populated mouse colony needs is another litter of young, hence the abortion. The odor of the strange male frees the egg from implantation. Thus smell serves as an agent of population control.

One of the strangest phenomena in nature is the chemical warfare carried on by certain insects. There is a species of ant that carries off the pupae of other ants as slaves to do their work. They get away with their bold venture by spraying the pupae's defenders with a fear-inducing chemical. So strong and effective is their chemical weapon that the defenders are afraid to return to their nest, even after the raiders have gone.

In American culture the olfactory sense has been suppressed more than any of the other senses. Compare Americans' reaction to body odor, for example, with that of Arab peoples. An Arab bridegroom will sometimes send his friends to "smell" the bride-to-be. Should they report sensing body odors they associate with discontent, unhappiness, or laziness, the groom may call off the wedding. Whereas Americans use visual cues to set social distance, Arabs employ olfactory cues. When an Arab is close enough to smell the natural body and breath odors of another person, he knows that he is at the proper social distance. Without smell he would feel "left out" and alienated. Americans, on the other hand, are usually offended if acquaintances move in so close to them that breath and body odors are detected.

Each human being is surrounded by a small haze of odor, and the evidence at present seems to indicate that no two people produce exactly the same odor. Researchers at the Illinois Institute of Technology are currently trying to develop "odor prints" of individuals. Should they succeed, odor prints will take their place beside finger prints, voice prints, and lip prints as a positive means of identification.

Most authorities in the perfume industry agree that the built-in body chemistry of a person reacts in some unknown way with perfume, sometimes enhancing it, sometimes not. They have also noted that men and women have different odor acceptance levels. For example, at certain times women are so highly susceptible to musk, an ingredient of many perfumes, that they can smell one part in a billion. Men can hardly smell it at all. This strange phenomenon has led to the speculation that musk may be related to the female hormone estrogen.

In most cultures the odor zone is regarded as part of a person, neither pleasant nor unpleasant, but simply there. People smell and are smelled as part of the routine of daily living. In American culture, however, all natural body and breath odors seem to be suspect. Wherever possible they are replaced by synthetic odors produced in laboratories. Until fairly recent times, males were permitted more latitude than females with regard to natural odors. The concentrated efforts of the cosmetics industries have removed that latitude. The average American may now smell like lilacs, mint, moldy leather, or burnt incense. Few natural human odors are socially acceptable.

Certainly teachers need a higher tolerance for odors than most people. Young students are not yet slaves of the cosmetics industry so they will bring into the classroom the full spectrum of human odors. If a teacher is repelled, nonverbal behavior will reveal these feelings to students. Dedication in teachers means acknowledging the fact that people do not smell like lilacs. Healthy students smell wonderfully human. A teacher should not expect all students to smell exactly alike, for that is precisely the point of this discussion. Each is just a little different, and these differences provide a kind of information not available through any other medium. Doctors, dentists, and sanitation workers also have a culturally innate aversion to unpleasant odors. They do not let their biases interfere with their work, however.

If odors are powerful enough to cause pregnant mice to abort, it is not beyond reason to wonder if certain odors may facilitate or inhibit learning. Here is a field of study, practically untouched, to which enterprising teachers may make significant contributions. To what kind of odors do children respond favorably? Do responses differ with age and by sex? As students and teachers cross cultures in schools, what part, if any, do odors play in culture shock? Should a mathematics classroom smell exactly like a classroom for English literature? Are teachers curious enough to gather some of this information?

Olfactory information, in most other cultures, adds an important dimension to human interaction. Americans have unnecessarily impoverished themselves by suppressing or disguising natural odors. Undoubtedly there are many odors that ought to be controlled, but surely there are beneficial odors. How much and what kind of odor control is useful, especially in a school setting? The olfactory environment is largely unstudied and unused in American schools.

Visual Literacy

Communication by means of written signs and symbols is part of a larger field of study that has been called "visual literacy." In times past a literate person was one who could read and write with some acceptable degree of proficiency. Today the parameters of an even broader and more fundamental kind of literacy are slowly coming into focus. The researcher in visual literacy studies not only the fields of reading, writing, and other forms of visual communication, but also proposes to investigate how the human brain analyzes and organizes such information into logical, meaningful patterns. In its broadest sense, visual literacy encompasses the universe of visual phenomena and their meaning.

Hanging over the entire educational enterprise is the disturbing notion that schools begin the education of students with a cluster of second-order fundamentals and have not usually recognized nor taught the first-order fundamentals, which would make the former more intelligible to students. In short, schooling begins with reading and writing, when it should begin by teaching students how to process visual information.

For example, the relationship between seeing and looking is similar to the relationship between hearing and listening. Hearing is a mechanical process. Assuming no impairment of the hearing apparatus, everyone is born with the ability to hear proficiently, that is, each person is able to detect the wave characteristics associated with sound. But listening is an intellectual and perceptual process. It goes beyond mere hearing into the realm of decision-making based on meaning. A microphone hears; it is able to detect sound waves. But only an intelligent organism can listen because listening implies interpretation, introspection, memory, and a host of other concomitant skills and processes. It is safe to assume that students can hear with about equal proficiency. It is disastrous to assume that students are able to listen with similar proficiency. The spread in listening ability among students is at least as great as in any subject matter area.

Seeing, too, can be regarded as a mechanical process. Physiologically, each person is capable of detecting the same visual phenomena. Small deficiencies of sight are usually easily corrected. Looking, however, goes beyond seeing. To look means to detect, to discriminate, to interpret, and to make decisions about what is being seen. A camera sees, but only an intelligent organism can look. Looking implies a cluster of sub-skills, such as the ability to distinguish light from dark, the recognition of differences in brightness, the recognition of differences and similarities in shape, size, distance, height, and depth, the perception of movement, and many other skills. Needless to say, the spread in looking ability, or visual literacy, among students is also great.

It is possible to quarrel with the above descriptions and to say that what has been called "looking" is seeing, or vice versa. Although it would be helpful to standardize the vocabulary, the distinction is more than semantic. Two different sets of skills are involved. One set is a consequence of normal birth. The other must be learned, and that means that it must be taught in a logical way or learned randomly through trial and error. How each set is labeled is of small consequence. That one set of skills must be taught and learned in a systematic way, however, is of great significance to teachers.

Even a casual observation of public education as it is carried on today confirms some of our worst suspicions —many teachers at many grade levels fail to distinguish between hearing and listening and seeing and looking. They fail to recognize that listening and looking are learned skills and must be taught at the earliest possible time in students' careers. Teaching the eye and ear to process information in a logical, orderly fashion has been left to chance. The results are evident in classrooms all over the country.

Students fortunate enough to come from a background where they were introduced to games, puzzles, and other visual challenges, do better in school as a rule than students who were denied this early training. Psychologists label this a "rich sensory environment," but because most teachers have not operationalized this term in a systematic way, they have not brought about needed fundamental changes in early education. The skills required to put together a jig-saw puzzle, for example, skills involving size, shape, and placement discriminations, are exactly the same kind of skills needed to learn to read. It would follow, then, that students who begin their schooling with some degree of proficiency in visual literacy, everything else being equal, would enjoy a significant advantage over students who do not. Further, the implication is clear that "crash" programs in reading are doomed to failure unless they begin at the very beginning by teaching the fundamentals of visual literacy rather than word recognition.

A study completed at the Institute of Child Study of the University of Toronto lends considerable support to the above comments. The ability to perform simple graphic skills that were unrelated to I.Q. or comprehension accounted for nearly half the difference between the reading ability of good and poor readers in the early grades. Above the first grade, the inability to distinguish letter features and the arrangement of letters within words accounted for one-third to one-half of all the poor readers involved in the study. The study concluded that educators have underestimated individual differences in the ability to process visual features; they have over-estimated the role of whole words.

From the field of visual literacy, then, comes a set of basic skills that should become a significant part of the curriculum for early childhood education. This is the time for teaching the first-order fundamentals, the visual, auditory, tactile, and spatial skills and concepts upon which the second-order fundamentals of reading, writing, and observing are built. Implied also is a cluster of skills and concepts that, must be learned prior to reading remediation at any level. Without a solid foundation in the fundamentals of processing visual information, it is difficult to see how reading programs for poor readers can have significant success at all.

Many of the discriminations identified throughout this book depend on a high degree of visual literacy. To identify and interpret spatial arrangements, postural and gesturial movements, facial expressions, and similar behavior call for an unusual ability to detect, isolate, and interpret visual cues. A teacher's success will be determined in large part by his proficiency levels of visual literacy.

Visual literacy branches off into areas that may be unknown to teachers but which nevertheless could have some important implications. There is, for example, an embryonic field called graphotherapy that has been derived from the controversial field of graphology. Graphology purports to give personality information through an analysis of the structural features of handwriting.

Graphotherapy goes a step further. It proposes to change personality by imitating and practicing the handwriting of people with desired personality characteristics. Does it work? The guarded enthusiasm of some psychiatrists and psychologists is encouraging, but more evidence is needed.

Then there are the kinetic drawings of children. Most teachers are familiar with the well-known "draw a person" test of intelligence. Psychologists Howard Kaufman and Robert Burns have developed a new "draw a house" test for determining personality problems. By having children draw pictures of their families doing something, proponents of this test believe they can identify and treat certain kinds of emotional disorders. For example, children who feel neglected by the family frequently draw mother cleaning house and father driving off to work. Tough, demanding fathers are often depicted mowing the lawn or chopping wood. Girls who both love and hate their mothers tend to draw cats in their pictures. Children who feel isolated may draw a house in cross section with each member of the family in his own room doing separate things.

The validity of these and similar fields of study has not been established to everyone's satisfaction, of course. They do point to new avenues of exploration and, if nothing else, they hint at a kind of information that may become available in the future. The important point for teachers to consider, however, is that visual literacy is a new and important field of study, which at last is coming to grips with some fundamental skills that all students need to understand basic curriculum subjects. Specifically, visual literacy challenges teachers to develop materials and implement strategies for teaching children how to process visual information in a logical, orderly fashion, and at an early age.

Vocal Information

Separate and apart from speech is a class of message-bearing sounds that has been called vocal information. In fact, speech is merely a vehicle for this sort of information. Sometimes it is called "vocal tone" or "intonation," but by whatever name it is known, the importance of vocal information in human interaction is beyond doubt. In fact, whenever there is a conflict between vocal and verbal information, the listener will disregard the verbal and heed the vocal. Suppose a second-grade teacher is attempting, verbally, to convince students of the importance of daily exercise. Should the students detect vocal cues of tone and inflection that contradict the teacher's words, students may listen politely but will disregard the words.

Sometimes a teacher may, for effect, deliberately contradict verbal information with vocal cues. To a student who has failed an exam, a teacher may say, "Well, that was certainly a major catastrophe." But the way in which the remark is made carries the real message. "Don't give up; the exam was not that important."

Subconscious vocal tone may add weight to or subtract from the credibility of verbal utterances. Teachers whose vocal cues tend to contradict their verbal messages will find their credibility with students steadily diminishing. Even herring gulls can detect a phony when they hear one. Gulls assign different weights to the alarm calls of individuals in the flock. When some individuals call, other members merely look up. When others call, however, the whole flock takes flight. Certainly human students experience little difficulty in learning how much weight to assign various teachers' cries of alarm.

At the present level of understanding, little more can be done than to alert teachers to the importance of vocal information in verbal interaction with students. In the absence of much needed data regarding this particular dimension of nonverbal communication, teachers would be well-advised to be sincere in their verbal dealings with students and to approach their job in a positive, helpful way. Positive intonation, for example, has been shown to have a dramatic effect on children's learning. Disadvantaged children in particular, tend to respond most favorably to positive, encouraging vocal tones. Once again, here is a field of study, virtually untouched, to which teachers can make a significant and lasting contribution.

What's in a Name

To complete this exploration of nonverbal languages, a final wonder remains—first names. The advent of a new baby into a household is cause for a number of important decisions, not the least of which is naming the baby. In the past, parents simply picked out a name that suited their fancy, and forever after, barring legal procedures to change it, the baby and his name were inseparable.

Teachers know that young children identify strongly with their first names. Through the crucial years of early childhood his first name is the child's handle on reality. Schools are full of Tommys, Carols, Billys, and Lucys whose only claim to existence is their first name. What happens when a child with an unusual first name enters school?

First of all, he begins to realize that his name is different almost as soon as he comes into contact with other children. He is his name. When other children laugh at his name, they are laughing at him. It must be a strange name or classmates would not make fun of it. Therefore, he must be strange, and strange people do strange things. A psychologist at Loyola University in Chicago has established that there are four times as many psychotic individuals with unusual names. A study of Harvard undergraduate students found that young people with unusual names are more likely to fail and become neurotic than students with run-of-the-mill names. Many young people grow to hate the names foisted on them by unthinking parents. It is a short step from hating one's name to hating one's self.

Certainly the warning flag is up for young parents on the verge of naming new offspring. There is more to a name than has been realized. Even ordinary names seem to carry with them certain kinds of behavior patterns. A researcher at the University of Bristol in England has been studying girls' names and their relationship to the personalities of the girls who hold the names. Some of his findings are strange and disturbing. Elizabeth is usually likeable and intelligent. Doris tends to be overweight, gossipy, and not too bright. Susan is just about average, one of the crowd. He concludes that names do have some effect on personality.

What kinds of messages do names carry? How does a human being interact with his own name? Are names the best way to identify people? In this age of electronic data processing, it is much easier and more reliable to reduce people to numbers. Most people are not too enthusiastic about this sort of depersonalization, even though it may facilitate the flow of information. But on the other hand, if names affect personality, do parents have the right to disadvantage their own children in the cradle by saddling them with strange and unusual names? As new generations pass through their classrooms, perhaps teachers will help students identify and resolve this and other problems that other generations never had to face.

Perhaps, many teachers will leave this discussion of nonverbal communication in the classroom with both a sense of wonder and frustration. They have been asked to learn too much in too little time. But there is so much more to be learned. Beyond the words of human beings there is a world of communication whose extent and variety has only begun to be explored. Where tomorrow's research will lead, no one knows. The prospects are exciting, however, and of particular interest to teachers, whose work is intimately involved with human communication.

To the interested teacher who wishes to explore further the implications of nonverbal communication for teaching, *The Challenge of Nonverbal Awareness* and *Teaching is Communication* are especially recommended. Dr. Charles Galloway of Ohio State University, author and editor of these publications, is an active student of nonverbal behavior whose interest in the field goes back many years. And to teachers everywhere this challenge is offered—contribute to this growing body of information. Push back the frontiers of knowledge in an area that has so much to offer the teaching profession.

FOR FURTHER READING

Arnheim, Rudof. *Visual Thinking.* University of California Press, 1971.

Audiovisual Instruction, vol. 17, no. 5, May 1972. (The theme of this issue is visual literacy).

Frymier, Jack R., and Charles H. Galloway, eds. *The Challenge of Nonverbal Awareness. Theory Into Practice: Journal of the College of Education.* Columbus: Ohio State University, vol. x, no. 4, October 1971.

Galloway, Charles H. *Teaching is Communication* (Bulletin No. 29). Washington D.C.: Association for Student Teaching, National Education Association, 1970.

Henley, Arthur. "Your Child's Name Could Mark Him for Failure." *Ladies Home Journal,* June 1970, pp. 137–9.

Kaufman, S. Howard, and Robert C. Burns. *Kinetic Family Drawings.* New York: Bruner/Mazel, 1970.

Luce, Gay Gaer. *Body Time: Physiological Rhythms and Social Stress.* New York: Pantheon, 1971.

Mehrabian, Albert. "Communication Without Words." *Psychology Today,* vol. 2, no. 4, Sept. 1968, pp. 53–5.

Plaffman, Carl, ed. *Olfaction and Taste: Proceedings of the Third International Symposium.* New York: Rockefeller University Press, 1970.

Reinert, Jeanne. "What Your Sense of Time Tells About You." *Science Digest,* vol. 69, no. 6, June 1971, pp. 8–12.

Report on Educational Research. Washington, D.C.: Capital Publications, Suite G42, 2430 Pennsylvania Ave:, October 13, 1971.

Williams, Clarence M., and John L. Debes, eds. *Visual Literacy: Proceedings of the First National Conference.* New York: Pitman, 1970.

Wilson, Edward O. "Pheromones." Reprinted from *Scientific American.* San Francisco: W. H. Freeman, 1963.

Yaker, Henri, et al., eds. *The Future of Time.* Garden City, N.Y.: Doubleday, 1971.